# THE CHURCH IN A

# PAGAN SOCIETY

# ~LUMINAIRE STUDIES~

# THE CHURCH IN A

# PAGAN SOCIETY

## Studies in 1 CORINTHIANS

### DAVID EWERT

Personal Response Sections by
Dennis and Nancy Becker

**Kindred Press**

Winnipeg, MB, Canada                    Hillsboro, KS, U.S.A.

THE CHURCH IN A PAGAN SOCIETY

Scripture taken from the HOLY BIBLE: NEW INTERNATIONAL VERSION.
Copyright 1973, 1978, 1984 by the International Bible Society. Used by permission
of Zondervan Bible Publishers.

Cover Design by Lee Toews, TS Design Associates, Winnipeg, Manitoba.

Printed in Canada by The Christian Press, Winnipeg.

International Standard Book Number: 0-919797-43-1

To the late Bernard W. Sawatzky, instructor at the Coaldale Bible School, who by his love and patience won me for the cause of the Kingdom.

# Foreword

When the editor of the Mennonite Brethren Herald six years ago asked for a series of expositions of Paul's first letter to the Corinthians no thought was given to the publishing of these articles in book form. However, through the encouragement of Gilbert Brandt, coordinator of publications for the Mennonite Brethren Church, the author agreed to have these twenty-five articles on I Corinthians put together into one volume.

This series of studies, published in the Mennonite Brethren Herald, beginning October 10, 1980, and ending January 14, 1983, appear in this book essentially as they were published with only a few minor corrections. A short list of commentaries on I Corinthians is given at the end for those who wish to pursue the study of this epistle in greater depth.

The chapters of this volume are designed for Bible study groups who may find some of the standard commentaries a bit too heavy or too bulky. Also, the busy preacher may find help in these chapters in his effort to preach through I Corinthians. Moreover, the brevity of the chapters in this volume may be useful to those individual believers who practice daily Bible study (may their tribe increase).

The author's interest in I Corinthians was profoundly stimulated when, thirty years ago, the third-year Greek class at seminary in Toronto waded through this epistle. Later it became his good fortune to teach I Corinthians to both college and seminary classes. Some twenty years ago the author, together with Drs. J.A. Toews and F.C. Peters, worked his way through I Corinthians at the annual Elmwood Bible Conference in Winnipeg. These sermons, preached in German and edited by H.F. Klassen, were published in 1964 by The Christian Press under the title: *Das ernste Ringen um die reine Gemeinde.*

Every Bible reader or teacher of the Word who wrestles with the question of how the church is to live in our pagan society, will turn again and again to I Corinthians. Here we discover how Paul tried to overcome dissension in the Body of Christ; here we watch him do battle with immorality and all that degrades the human body; here we learn how he felt about Christians getting even with each other before the courts.

For instruction on the conjugal relationship of husband and wife, on the tragedy of divorce and remarriage, the problem of believer/unbeliever marriages, we quickly turn to I Corinthians. We may not face the question of eating meat dedicated to idols, but we still have to grapple with questions of conscience. The tension between liberty and license is very acutely present in the church today, not to mention the current debate about the place of the woman in the church. In such areas we need to take seriously Paul's guidance.

When it comes to public worship and the use of spiritual gifts, I Corinthians is very relevant. Moreover, without I Corinthians 13, that magnificent chapter on love, and I Corinthians 15, which lights up our life after death so brilliantly, we would be much the poorer.

May I invite the reader, then, to walk with me once again through I Corinthians — a book inspired by the Holy Spirit and, therefore, perennially fresh and meaningful and authoritative.

David Ewert

# TABLE OF CONTENTS

# CHAPTER ONE

## Saints in Corinth

*Paul, called to be an apostle of Christ Jesus by the will of God, and our brother Sosthenes, To the church of God in Corinth, to those sanctified in Christ Jesus and called to be holy, together with all those everywhere who call on the name of our Lord Jesus Christ — their Lord and ours: Grace and peace to you from God our Father and the Lord Jesus Christ.*

*I always thank God for you because of his grace given you in Christ Jesus. For in him you have been enriched in every way — in all your speaking and in all your knowledge — because our testimony about Christ was confirmed in you. Therefore you do not lack any spiritual gift as you eagerly wait for our Lord Jesus Christ to be revealed. He will keep you strong to the end, so that you will be blameless on the day of our Lord Jesus Christ. God, who has called you into fellowship with his Son Jesus Christ our Lord, is faithful (I Corinthians 1:1-9).*

An earlier letter of Paul to the Corinthians has not survived (5:9), and so we call this epistle First Corinthians. We know of at least two other letters to the Corinthians: the "letter of anguish" (II Cor. 2:4) and our Second Corinthians.

After establishing the church in Corinth, Paul and his companions returned to Antioch, their home base. On his so-called "third" missionary journey Paul settled in Ephesus for a protracted

1

ministry. Here he received word that things were not going too well in Corinth. Also, while in Ephesus, he received a letter from the Corinthian Church in which they asked him a number of questions.

Who delivered this letter to Paul is not known, but it may have been the three-man delegation that had come across the Aegean to visit Paul in Ephesus (16:17). First Corinthians is his response to these written and oral communications.

This letter touches upon a great variety of subjects and deals with them in orderly fashion. The topics discussed are intensely practical and are still very relevant for a church that lives and works in a pagan culture. We may not be overly concerned whether ladies should wear a head covering in church, but the relationship of male and female is a very live issue. Certainly the question of leadership in the church, sexual morality, spiritual gifts, and other subjects dealt with in this letter are still being asked. We invite you, therefore, to think with us about the issues with which Paul grappled in the first century.

In this our first meditation we want to focus on Paul's greeting (vv. 1-3), his thanksgiving (vv. 4-8) and his affirmation (v. 9).

## I. The Apostolic Greeting (1:1-3)

In keeping with the letter-style of the day, Paul begins his letter with a salutation (vv. 1-3). That's an older English word for the introductory words of a letter in which the readers are addressed with expressions of kind wishes and courtesy. Secular letters from Paul's day indicate that it was the custom to put the writer's name first at the head of the letter. Just as the Holy Spirit guided the biblical writers to use the language of the day, so the letter-form known to Paul's readers was not abolished just because it became the vehicle for the Word of God.

Paul introduces himself as an apostle of Christ Jesus, who was called into this ministry by God's sovereign will. He had heard this call on the Damascus Road. However, like Jeremiah of old (Jer. 1:5), God had his eye on Paul even before he was born (Gal. 1:15).

Associated with him in this salutation is Sosthenes, the brother. If this is the former ruler of the synagogue in Corinth (Acts 18:17) he must have become a Christian and was now with Paul. Whether he served Paul as secretary when the apostle dictated this letter (as was the custom) cannot be established, but he must have been well known to Paul's readers in Corinth. To be called a "brother" is a reminder to us that the church is a family, bound together not by blood-ties, but by the Spirit of God. Peter calls the church a "brotherhood" (I Pet. 5:9) — a term that no longer distinguishes men from women, but which has an ecclesiastical meaning.

The churches in the first century did not yet have denominational labels or other names but were known simply by their location. Paul writes to "the church of God being in Corinth" (v. 2). If it is God's church then it is under his protecting care, but also under his authority. Moreover, it does not belong to Paul, Cephas or anyone else (not to the pastor either), but to God. Nor is it simply a human organization; it is a divine institution; it is God's community.

This church, however, is located in rather earthy circumstances: in Corinth. The concept of an "invisible" church, which arose when the "visible" church became corrupt, is foreign to the New Testament. The church is an identifiable body of believers. One could, of course, not point to a steepled building on the corner of First Street and Second Avenue and say, "There's the Corinthian Church," for the word "church" signifies the new people of God. The early Christians met in the "living rooms" of church members for worship and fellowship and then scattered to pursue their daily work and to witness to their new faith in word and in deed.

With all the weaknesses and faults of this church Paul can still say of these young believers that they have been "sanctified in Christ Jesus." This means that they now belong to Christ and, because they are his, they have been separated from the evil and the profane. But like all the gifts of God's grace, this principial sanctification calls for a continuous human response. They have been "called to be saints" and so must strive after holiness. "Saints" is one of the most common designations of first century believers. Only later was the word used for the spiritual elite, such as the martyrs. In the first century, however, all members of the church went by this title. When God calls people to salvation, he calls them to holiness; they cannot have one without the other.

The complete autonomy of the local church is not a New Testament concept. Large urban churches are, perhaps, tempted more often than smaller churches to function rather independently of other churches. Paul reminds the Corinthians (who were not particularly outstanding in humility) that they are not the only saints around. They have been called to holiness "together with all those who in every place call on the name of the Lord" (v. 2). "Place" probably refers to the places where Christians in other cities worshipped (cf. I Tim. 2:8). In any case, the Corinthian Church was just one of a number of others, and the apostle asked (I Cor. 11:16) that it give heed to what other churches of God were doing.

As in all his letters Paul greets his readers with "grace to you and peace from God our Father and the Lord Jesus Christ" (v. 3). "Grace" is linguistically a variant of the common Greek greeting of "joy" (found in James 1:1, and meaning something like our "cheerio"). "Peace" ( shalom in Hebrew) is the well-known Semitic greeting. Paul seems to take the language of the street and "baptize" it into Christ. The words are deepened in meaning and together they come to form a peculiarly Christian greeting. How significant the order of the words is, is hard to say, but certainly there can be no peace, no wholeness in our lives until God's grace has covered our sin and our guilt.

## II. The Joyous Thanksgiving (1:4-8)

Paul normally follows his greeting with words of thanksgiving for the work of God's grace in the lives of his readers. Here, too, after the salutation (vv. 1-3), we have the thanksgiving (vv. 4-8). In spite of all the bad rumors Paul has heard about the Corinthians, he never forgets to thank God when he remembers the Corinthians in his prayers. What makes him particularly thankful is the fact that the grace of God not only brought salvation to his readers, but also that it enriched their lives by bestowing spiritual gifts upon them. Paul does not think lightly of these gifts. If only the Corinthians had also been rich in love. Paul will argue later (I Cor. 13) that without love spiritual gifts are useless.

The two gifts singled out in Paul's introduction are "speech" and "knowledge." "Knowledge" (*gnosis*) has reference to insight into God's ways. Evidently there were people in Corinth who had been given profound insight into the things of God. Such insights are all the more valuable when they are shared, and by God's grace even the ability to communicate the deep things of the Spirit had been graciously given to some Corinthians. It's always a pity when people with valuable insights do not seem to be able to share these with others. In Corinth both the gift of knowledge and of communication flourished.

The door to this spiritual wealth was opened up to the Corinthians when the gospel came to them. "The testimony of Christ" was confirmed among them (v. 6). Paul describes his message as a "witness" to Christ. After all, he did not originate the gospel; he received it and faithfully witnessed to its saving power.

Just what it means that the witness of Christ was "confirmed," is not quite clear. Does he mean that the gospel was planted firmly in their hearts? Or, was the gospel confirmed by the bestowal of spiritual gifts? In any case, the gospel had taken root in Corinth; the presence of the Corinthian Church was evidence of that.

Although the Corinthians did not lack in spiritual gifts — so necessary for their life and witness in the world — they were still in this age, living in the hope of the age to come. The gifts of the Spirit were but a foretaste of what awaited them in the eternal kingdom. They were now waiting for "the revelation of our Lord Jesus" (v. 7). As long as we are in this age our Lord is hidden from sight; we see him only by the eyes of faith. But when this age has run its course every eye shall see him. The Second Coming of Christ is described in a variety of ways in the NT; one of these designations is "the revelation." We should observe that the church is waiting not so much for certain events to happen, but for the coming of Jesus Christ. The person of our Lord and Savior overshadows all end-times events. Let us not allow any prognostications of the end ever remove our eyes from the hope of meeting our Lord.

This great and glorious event is not one that the readers need to fear, for the same Lord who called them to holiness and who enriched them with spiritual gifts will also establish them until the end. Not only was the witness of Christ confirmed among them (v. 6), but Christ himself will confirm them (v. 8). This is a reference to Christ's keeping power. He will complete the work he began "until the end."

On this day of the Lord, the day of Christ's revelation, the end, the believers are to appear "blameless." The word comes from the law-court and means something like "unimpeachable." Whereas all the saints will stand before the judgment seat of Christ, there is no condemnation for those in Christ Jesus.

## III. The Confident Affirmation (1:9)

Paul concludes his introduction with a strong affirmation: "God is faithful, by whom you are called into the fellowship of his Son, Jesus Christ our Lord" (v. 9). This is not the first time that Paul appeals to God's faithfulness as he thinks of the last day when Christ returns in glory (see I Thess. 5:24). God can be trusted to bring to conclusion the work of grace begun in the lives of the Corinthians — and in our life, too. He receives the credit for initiating the Christian life, and he will get all the credit for completing it.

The Christian life begins with the call of God in the gospel. Not only does God call us into "his kingdom and glory" (I Thess. 2:12), but, as Paul puts it here, into the fellowship with his Son. This personal relationship with Christ is made possible by the work of the Spirit. And whereas our fellowship with Christ may at times seem intimate and close, we are still far from home. Only when the gates of the eternal kingdom are opened for us will we enjoy fellowship with Christ in full measure. That's what makes heaven worth waiting for.

### *Personal Response*

1. *Paul was called by Jesus Christ (v. 1). Share your calls to follow Christ. These may be calls to salvation or to a particular ministry (either public or private).*
2. *Paul refers to Sosthenes as "our brother"; he was part of the family of God (v. 1). What does being a Christian family mean in practical terms? How is your church, Sunday school class, small group acting like a family?*
3. *The Corinthian believers were called "saints" or "holy" (v. 2). As we read I Corinthians, they hardly fit our common definitions of a saint. What are some characteristics of people whom you think of as "saints"?*
4. *If Paul were writing a prayer of thanksgiving about your church (vv. 4-8), for what would he be thankful?*
5. *The believers at Corinth were eagerly awaiting the return of Christ v. 7). How does the expectation of the return of Jesus affect your daily life?*
6. *God is faithful (v. 9). How do we recognize God's faithfulness? How does this affect our thinking about the future?*

# CHAPTER TWO

## A Divided Church

*I appeal to you, brothers, in the name of our Lord Jesus Christ, that all of you agree with one another so that there may be no divisions among you and that you may be perfectly united in mind and thought. My brothers, some from Chloe's household have informed me that there are quarrels among you. What I mean is this: One of you says, "I follow Paul"; another, "I follow Apollos"; another, "I follow Cephas"; still another, "I follow Christ."*

*Is Christ divided? Was Paul crucified for you? Were you baptized into the name of Paul? I am thankful that I did not baptize any of you except Crispus and Gaius, so no one can say that you were baptized into my name. (Yes, I also baptized the household of Stephanas; beyond that, I don't remember if I baptized anyone else.) For Christ did not send me to baptize, but to preach the gospel — not with words of human wisdom, lest the cross of Christ be emptied of its power (I Corinthians 1:10-17).*

After reading the introduction to Paul's letter one could easily jump to the conclusion that the Corinthian church was close to perfection. Established by an apostle, sanctified in Christ Jesus, richly blessed with spiritual gifts, called into fellowship with God's Son. Corinth (to use the modern idiom) "had it made."

As one reads on, however, one is shocked to discover that this church, which at first blush looked so ideal, had some ugly spots.

7

There was bad blood between cliques, factions, classes, parties in the church. The Corinthian church was torn by disunity; it was a divided church.

## I. Evidence of Disunity (vv. 10,11)

Paul was in Ephesus. Here word had reached him through Chloe's people that Corinth was torn by strife. We know nothing about this woman, other than that she had dependents (slaves or freed men), and so she must have been, perhaps like Lydia, a woman of means. Whether she was a Christian or not we do not know. She may have lived either in Corinth or in Ephesus. In any case, her servants knew about the rifts in the Corinthian congregation and brought this problem to Paul's attention.

Some argue they must have been Ephesians, otherwise Paul would not have identified them; for the Corinthians would hardly look kindly on members of their own ranks who brought the apostle up to date on their own foibles.

Be that as it may, Paul begins with a tender appeal to be done with quarreling. Not only the verb "beseech" but also the word "brothers" (found 35 times in I Corinthians) carries with it a note of tenderness. He is not cracking the whip over their heads but is pleading with them to restore the unity of the Spirit in Corinth. Moreover, Paul begs them "by the name of the Lord Jesus" to mend the tears in the body of Christ (the Greek word *schisma* means rip, tear, split, crack, division). The name of Jesus has always drawn Christians together in a deeper and powerful way.

How deep the splits in Corinth were is not known. Could they still worship together, or did the different parties hive themselves off into different house churches? How sad when the church becomes fractured. In the shadow of the cross Jesus prayed that the future church might be one "so that the world may believe that thou hast sent me" (Jn. 17:21). A quarreling church loses its strength to witness to the world.

We recognize, of course, that when a church becomes corrupt, a division may be necessary to preserve the integrity of the gospel. We think, for example, of the Protestant Reformation.

Frequently I hear the song, "We are one in the Spirit, We are one in the Lord... *And we pray that all unity may one day be restored....*" What do we mean when we sing that?

But let us look, next, at the nature of the disunity at Corinth.

## II. Nature of Division (v. 12)

One person in the Corinthian congregation said he belonged to Paul, another, he belonged to Apollos, still another, he belonged to Cephas. Christians were taking up sides by rallying around famous leaders.

As far as we know the divisions in Corinth were not caused by doctrinal disputes. Those who lifted Paul's banner high (something he disapproved of) may have been the church's charter members, that nucleus with which the church began. It is often hard for charter members of a congregation to view those who have come into the church later as having equal status (especially when charter members must relinquish leadership positions).

It could also be that Paul's fans were comprised of the Gentile Christians in the church, in contrast to the Jewish party that rallied around Cephas.

That some should carry the banner of Apollos need not surprise us, either. This fiery preacher from Alexandria must have mesmerized his audience at numerous occasions and his followers may have claimed that neither Paul nor Cephas could hold a candle to Apollos. He may even have practiced the allegorical interpretation of the Old Testament — something for which Alexandria came to be known. Whether Peter had ever visited Corinth is not known, but as a pillar apostle of the Jerusalem mother-church he was held in high respect. Interestingly, Paul almost without exception calls him by his Aramaic nickname "Cephas."

Perhaps the most difficult group in Corinth was the "Christ party." These were possibly the spiritually elite. They wouldn't think of carrying human labels, but their spiritual pride made cooperation with others quite impossible. Some think they may have been Gnostic in tendency and that they claimed to have spiritual insights that others did not have and, therefore, felt themselves superior to the rest. There's nothing wrong with saying "I belong to Christ." Indeed, if one can't say that, one can hardly claim the name Christian. But if one says it with a tone that is exclusive, suggesting that one belongs to Christ as others do not, then spiritual pride creates a rift between believers.

It is possible, however, that there were only three groups and that the confession "But I am of Christ" is Paul's own response to all this party-strife. In fact, it has been suggested that some scribe later copying this letter read all these rallying calls and in protest wrote in the margin: "But I belong to Christ" — a comment that was then later incorporated into the text of the letter. There is, however, no manuscript evidence for this. In any case, Paul condemns all these divisions.

It would be overly simplistic to apply Paul's wholesale condemnation of these Corinthian cliques to the denominational scene today. Many Protestant denominations have been historically and culturally determined (Scottish Presbyterians, Finnish Lutherans, German Baptists, Swiss Mennonites), although there may also be deep theological differences. Appreciation for other denominations does not mean a lack of loyalty to one's own. In fact, only those who know what their own church believes, who have accepted its teachings and have thrown in their lot with their denomination "for better or for worse," can truly appreciate what God is doing in other denominations without feeling threatened.

Paul addresses himself in our passage to the disunity of a local congregation, and that is where disunity is often felt most acutely. But, given the fact that history has bequeathed a multiplicity of denominations upon us, is it not just as pitiful to see a denomination torn by petty jealousies and rivalries, misunderstandings, accusations, suspicions, even hatreds and animosities? Is Christ divided in your church?

### III. Absurdity of Divisions (vv. 13-17)

With a series of rhetorical questions Paul hammers home the absurdity of divisions among believers who claim to be the followers of the Christ who has forgiven them all. In Corinth it appeared as if Christ was in fact divided. Was Paul crucified for the Corinthians? No, then he would be their Savior. Were they baptized in Paul's name? No! All believers are baptized in Christ's name and so belong to him, not to the baptizer (Paul uses himself as example to shield his colleagues).

A pioneer missionary can hardly avoid baptizing some of the first converts when a church is born, and so Paul admits that he baptized a few people: Crispus, Gaius, and (he almost forgot) also the household of Stephanus. (Those who argue that this included the babies should be reminded that the household of Stephanus devoted itself to the service of the saints, I Cor. 16:15.) However, Paul allowed others to do the baptizing once the church had been established, lest he tie his converts to his own apron strings. The apostles were not pastors of churches; they were church planters, and so they left the pastoral functions to the leaders of the churches they established.

Missionary Jacob Franz found one of the Indian churches in the Chaco divided. Those baptized by Franz felt superior to those baptized by their own leaders. So he called a meeting at which he asked: "Did I use my name when I baptized you?" The answer was no! "Whose name did I use?" "Christ's." "And whose name did your leaders use?" "Also Christ's." "Then there can't be any difference." No, indeed, then all strife must cease and we must "welcome one another...as Christ has welcomed us (you)" (Rom. 15:7).

George Whitefield, the great English evangelist of the 18th century, was preaching in Philadelphia and in the course of his message apostrophized: "Father Abraham, whom have you in heaven? Any Episcopalians? No! Any Presbyterians? No! Have you any Methodists? No, no, no! Whom have you there? We don't know those names here. All who are here are Christians — believers in Christ — people who have overcome by the blood of the Lamb and the word of his testimony. Oh, is this the case, then God help us; God help us all, to forget party names and to become Christians in deed and in truth."

### Personal Response

1. *Paul is concerned about divisions in the church (v. 10). Think about your local church in relationship to other local churches and/or denominations. How is your church like others? How is it different? In what do you agree? In what do you disagree? In what areas can you work together?*
2. *What is the basis of our fellowship with other believers? What is the minimum statement of faith that we cannot give up for the sake of fellowship (v. 10)?*
3. *How can we disagree with other people but still find fellowship with them?*

4. Members of the Corinthian church gave allegiance to various individuals (v. 12). To whom or what might we give allegiance and thus bring division in the church?
5. What does it mean to "preach the gospel" (v. 17)?

# CHAPTER THREE

## The Paradoxes in God's Ways

*For the message of the cross is foolishness to those who are perishing, but to us who are being saved it is the power of God. For it is written: "I will destroy the wisdom of the wise; the intelligence of the intelligent I will frustrate."*

*Where is the wise man? Where is the scholar? Where is the philosopher of this age? Has not God made foolish the wisdom of the world? For since in the wisdom of God the world through its wisdom did not know him, God was pleased through the foolishness of what was preached to save those who believe. Jews demand miraculous signs and Greeks look for wisdom, but we preach Christ crucified: a stumbling block to Jews and foolishness to Gentiles, but to those whom God has called, both Jews and Greeks, Christ the power of God and the wisdom of God. For the foolishness of God is wiser than man's wisdom, and the weakness of God is stronger than man's strength.*

*Brothers, think of what you were when you were called. Not many of you were wise by human standards; not many were influential; not many were of noble birth. But God chose the foolish things of the world to shame the wise; God chose the weak things of the world to shame the strong. He chose the lowly things of this world and the despised things — and the things that are not — to nullify the things that are, so that no one may boast before him. It is because of him that you are in Christ Jesus, who has become for us*

> *wisdom from God — that is, our righteousness, holiness and*
> *redemption. Therefore, as it is written: "let him who boasts boast*
> *in the Lord."*
>     *When I came to you, brothers, I did not come with eloquence*
> *or superior wisdom as I proclaimed to you the testimony about God.*
> *For I resolved to know nothing while I was with you except Jesus*
> *Christ and him crucified. I came to you in weakness and fear, and*
> *with much trembling. My message and my preaching were not with*
> *wise and persuasive words, but with a demonstration of the Spirit's*
> *power, so that your faith might not rest on men's wisdom, but on*
> *God's power (I Corinthians 1:18-2:5).*

The Corinthians were quarreling over leaders. They pitted Paul against Apollos, Apollos against Cephas, Cephas against Paul, and the church was divided over which of these was the greatest. This comparison of leaders came from a fundamental misunderstanding of the nature of the ministry.

The Corinthians looked at Christian teachers and ministers through human eyes; they were employing human measuring sticks. In God's Kingdom, however, other standards are employed. God's ways are often quite contrary to man's, and so, in an attempt to overcome the party spirit in Corinth, the apostle elaborates on the paradoxes in God's ways. The word "paradox" comes into English from the Greek and means that which is contrary to opinion, the unexpected, the strange. In the passage before us we shall see how God often works completely contrary to human expectations.

### I. Human Wisdom and Divine Foolishness (1:18-25)

"For the word of the cross is foolishness to those who are perishing, but to us who are being saved it is the power of God" (v. 18). The cross was for Paul the burning center of salvation history. At the heart of the gospel is the story of Christ's death, and the good news is that by that unspeakable tragedy salvation has come to man.

To those who are on the way to eternal ruin such a message is plainly foolishness. How can the horrible death of an insignificant Galilean offer deliverance from the power of sin and Satan and death? It makes no sense. Had Jesus been divine, charged Celsus, an early critic of Christianity, he would have disappeared from the cross rather than submitting to the shame and the insults heaped on him. The only conclusion Celsus came to was that the Christian message is blatant nonsense.

By contrast, those who respond to the gospel in faith and obedience discover its liberating power. This reminds Paul of a passage in Isaiah 29:14 where, in the face of the Assyrian invasion, God put the worldly statesmanship of Judah to shame. By intervening and delivering Judah in an unexpected way, God destroyed the wisdom of the wise and thwarted the cleverness of the clever (v. 19). This he also did by saving the world through a man who hung on a shameful cross.

Let us make sure that we do not misunderstand the apostle's denunciation of human wisdom. The wisdom Paul condemns is man's desire to save himself by his own ingenuity. Paul is not down-grading education. The uneducated are just as loath to look to the cross for salvation as the educated. Learning does not save, but neither does ignorance. Both the learned and the unlearned would much rather look for salvation elsewhere. Non-Christian religions are convenient ways of circumventing the cross. Secular ideologies are more appealing than the word from the cross. But all such alternatives are "the wisdom of this world" (v. 20) which God set aside when he decided to save mankind by the cross.

Since the world had not come to know God by its own wisdom, by its own schemes of redemption, God in his eternal wisdom decreed that he would save those who believe through "the foolishness of preaching" (v. 21). Paul is not saying that "preaching" is a foolish exercise (although some seem to think so). Also, as A.T. Robertson points out, "the foolishness of preaching" does not mean "the preaching of foolishness" (sad to say there has been more of that than we need). What Paul means is that the message of the gospel which proclaims redemption by the death of Jesus on a gibbet outside Jerusalem, is folly to both Jew and Gentile.

The Jew expected the Messiah to demonstrate his power by a magnificent display of signs. Jesus had done great signs, but he died in shame. To accept him as Messiah was blasphemous, for it stood written that everyone who hangs upon a tree is an accursed one of God (Deut. 21:23). The Greek might ask: How could anyone who didn't have enough wit to save himself from so ghastly a death or who wasn't an exponent of wisdom, claim to be a deliverer of mankind (vv. 22, 23)?

But over against this human stubbornness and perverseness stand those who are "called" (who hear God's invitation in the gospel and accept it). These experience the power of God in deliverance from sin, and now marvel at the wisdom of God (v. 24). How strange the ways of God!

## II. Human Insignificance and Divine Grace (1:26-31)

The paradox of God's ways is seen not only in the strange manner in which God carried out redemption, but also by the kind of people he calls by the gospel. The composition of the Corinthian church was a good illustration of how God cuts across all standards of human greatness. There were relatively few converts from the worldly wise, the powerful, or the nobility (v. 26).

Most of Paul's converts at Corinth seem to have come from the lower classes. The second century critic of Christianity, Celsus, despised the new faith because there were in the church "wool dressers, cobblers and fullers, the most uneducated and vulgar persons." But it was the glory of the church that it made people who amounted to nothing in society (particularly the slaves) into sons and daughters of God with dignity and worth. There were of course also converts from the upper crust of society (Erastus, the city treasurer, Paul's host, belonged to the Corinthian church), but they were in the minority. Selina, Countess of Huntingdon, was always grateful for the letter "m" in the word "many." Paul said "not many" of the highborn were called; he did not say "not any." At the beginning of the second century Pliny, the governor of Bithynia, could write to the emperor Trajan about the Christians and say that they came from every rank in society.

The point that Paul is making is that cultural, economic and political advantages play no role in God's plan of salvation. Everyone stands bankrupt before God and must repent and receive his grace like a child in order to experience "the power of God unto salvation." Employer and employee, parent and child, ruler and subject, learned and unlearned, rich and poor must all come to Christ in the same way.

And what is true of salvation holds also for service. While God uses those who are academically trained for certain kinds of ministry (one might think of Luther, Calvin, Grebel, Spener, Wesley and others), he uses also the cobbler, William Carey, and the mill-worker, David Livingstone. God simply does not follow human standards when he calls people into the kingdom and into his service.

The reason God cuts clean across all human standards of greatness, across all social classes, is so that no human being should boast in the presence of God (v. 29). And when God calls the oppressed, the despised, the poor into his kingdom, he gives us an object lesson of his grace. What a person is by birth, by training, by possession, by class, does not recommend him to God. Salvation comes alone as a gift from Christ, whose death on the cross was a display of divine wisdom, for in him we now have righteousness, sanctification and redemption (v. 30).

Every desire to boast is thereby cut off. Salvation by the cross shuts our arrogant mouths. On the other hand, it opens our mouths to boast in the Lord. And that is in keeping with Jeremiah's exhortation, "Let him who boasts, boast in the Lord" (v. 31).

### III. Human Weakness and Divine Power (2:1-5)

If God acts contrary to human wisdom in his saving activity, then the manner in which the gospel is preached is also affected by this principle. Paul had recognized this and so when he faced Corinth, a bastion of wickedness, he decided (as he often must have done) that he would not proclaim the gospel with "lofty words of wisdom" (v. 1).

Paul is not despising eloquence per se. There is no merit in presenting the gospel in a chaotic fashion and in bad English. It is true, as Alan Cole of Sydney puts it, that "God sometimes blesses a poor exegesis of a bad translation of a doubtful reading of an obscure verse of a minor prophet," but he does that in spite of the limitations of the sermon, not because of them.

Paul knew that God's saving power lay not in highfalutin language, but in the content of the gospel. The heart of the gospel, as he explains, is "Jesus Christ and him crucified" (v. 2), and not human schemes of salvation, or human wisdom. We should not understand this as a narrow, restricted theme, for the cross, by implication, suggests the whole sweep of redemption history. For Jews the message of the cross meant that Jesus, who was crucified, was under God's curse, and for Gentiles it meant that Jesus was a criminal, done to death by Roman justice. We can see, then, why the passion story of the gospels, in which it is made clear that the criminal charges brought against him were totally without foundation, was given such a prominent place in early preaching.

If then, the power to save people lies not in the preacher but in the message, empowered by the Spirit, we are not surprised to hear that Paul felt weak and shaky as he faced pagan Corinth (v. 31). Paul was overcome by feelings of personal inadequacy (not a bad mood for preaching). The apostle had by now preached for some 15 years, but he never felt quite "up to it." William Barclay of Scotland admitted before his death that although he had preached for some 40 years, preaching still frightened him. And he makes the comment: "It is, I think, in fact true, that, if a man can enter a pulpit without turning a hair, then it is time that he stopped entering it."

Paul was convinced that he could not deliver anyone from sin and death through persuasive arguments (although he spoke persuasively no doubt). The power of the message lay not in rational arguments; even less in emotional fervor (although enthusiasm is not unimportant). It lay, rather, in the "demonstration of the Spirit and power" (v. 4). "Spirit" and "power" are found so often as a word pair in the New Testament that at times they are almost interchangeable.

After a preacher of the gospel has prepared his message well, and after he has delivered it in the best way that he is capable of, he should know that unless God's Spirit takes the word and applies it to the hearts of the hearers his words are of little effect. We are not surprised then to hear that C.H. Spurgeon frequently mumbled to himself as he walked to the pulpit: "I believe in the Holy Spirit."

Paul had come to see that a response by his hearers, based on rational arguments and persuasive rhetoric, could not create a living faith. Only God who works by his Spirit can infuse new life into the repentant sinner who responds to the gospel. Someone who has been talked into believing in Jesus can easily be talked out of it again by someone who is more persuasive. But where faith rests in the power of God (v.5), it is genuine and deep. And this power of God is at work through the Holy Spirit when the gospel is proclaimed.

By now, it seems, Paul has forgotten about the party-strife in Corinth. The contrast between God's inscrutable ways and human wisdom continues to absorb him. But if his readers can be convinced that in God's kingdom other than human standards obtain, they will have to stop squabbling over the church's teachers.

### Personal Response

1. *Paul brought the gospel to Corinth in simplicity, but also in power (v. 2:4). When we think of evangelism and church growth, we often think of dynamic or persuasive ways of presenting the gospel or to portray a slick, entertaining view of the church. Identify some of these ways.*
2. *What will attract people to Christ and to the church that does not fall under the category of "worldly wisdom"?*
3. *How can the church demonstrate that the gospel is for both those whom the world considers prominent and important and those whom the world considers common?*
4. *Outline a basic presentation of the gospel message.*

# CHAPTER FOUR

## The Wisdom of God

*We do, however, speak a message of wisdom among the mature, but not the wisdom of this age or of the rulers of this age, who are coming to nothing. No, we speak of God's secret wisdom, a wisdom that has been hidden and that God destined for our glory before time began. None of the rulers of this age understood it, for if they had, they would not have crucified the Lord of glory. However, as it is written: "No eye has seen, no ear has heard, no mind has conceived what God has prepared for those who love him" — but God has revealed it to us by his Spirit.*

*The Spirit searches all things even the deep things of God. For whom among men knows the thoughts of a man except the man's spirit within him? In the same way no one knows the thoughts of God except the Spirit of God. We have not received the spirit of the world but the Spirit who is from God, that we may understand what God has freely given us. This is what we speak, not in words taught us by human wisdom but in words taught by the Spirit, expressing spiritual truths in spiritual words. The man without the Spirit does not accept the things that come from the Spirit of God, for they are foolishness to him, and he cannot understand them, because they are spiritually discerned. The spiritual man makes judgments about all things, but he himself is not subject to any man's judgment: "For who has known the mind of the Lord that he may instruct him?" But we have the mind of Christ.*

21

> *Brothers, I could not address you as spiritual but as worldly —*
> *mere infants in Christ. I gave you milk, not solid food, for you were*
> *not yet ready for it. Indeed, you are still not ready. You are still*
> *worldly. For since there is jealousy and quarreling among you, are*
> *you not worldly? Are you not acting like mere men? For when one*
> *says, "I follow Paul," and another, "I follow Apollos," are you not*
> *mere men? (I Corinthians 2:6-3:4).*

The word "wisdom" is used by Paul in both a negative and a positive sense. Human wisdom is seen in man's desire to live independently of God, in his rejection of God's offer of salvation through the cross, and in his evaluation of spiritual and ethical matters by secular standards.

There is, however, another kind of wisdom, namely divine wisdom — a wisdom which looks rather foolish in the eyes of the world. It is seen in the manner in which God accomplishes our redemption (by the cross). True wisdom is seen also in God's revelation of his saving purposes to man. Let us follow Paul in his development of this theme!

## I. Character of Divine Wisdom (2:6-8)

From Paul's rejection of human wisdom in his missionary activity the readers could have concluded that Paul's message lacked content. Or, after hearing Apollos, some may have dismissed Paul's teaching as elementary. The apostle explains, therefore, that he can go deeper, too, if the audience is ready for it. "Among the mature we do impart wisdom" (v. 6). He will explain later (3:1ff.) why he had not ploughed as deep at Corinth as he might have wished to.

The mature (*teleioi*) are believers who have learned the basic elements of the gospel and have gone on to deeper things. Paul has no desire to stratify the church by labelling some members as mature and others as immature. The fact of the matter is, however, that some believers capture more quickly and more profoundly the implications of the gospel for themselves and for the life of the church. Spiritual maturity, incidentally, is not determined simply by intelligence but, as we shall see, by love.

The wisdom of God, which a mature Christian can easily grasp, is not a "wisdom of this age or of the rulers of this age, who are doomed to pass away." In Jewish thought there were basically two ages: the present age and the age to come. This present age was thought of as an evil age (Gal. 1:4). God's wisdom, says Paul, does not originate in this present age. Such wisdom is man-centered and is marked by rebellion against God. This age is under the dominion of supernatural evil powers that control the current climate of opinion.

It is often not recognized sufficiently that what goes for the Canadian or American "way of life," call it our "culture" if you will, is strongly under the influence of the "god of this age," and believers need the whole armor of God to stand against "the world rulers of the present darkness" (Eph. 6:12). Since Christ defeated these evil powers at the cross their demise is only a matter of time.

The wisdom which Paul proclaims is a "hidden" wisdom. It is a "mystery"! Mystery, however, does not mean that God's wisdom is not understood. Rather, it is a wisdom which only God can disclose. Man can't discover it on his own. In Christ that wisdom which had been hidden for ages in God has now been manifested and so the word "mystery" comes to be an equivalent for divine revelation. The preaching of the cross is the hidden wisdom which God "decreed before the ages for our glorification" (v. 7). Already in this age the believer has a foretaste of what awaits him in glory.

The rulers of this age, however, do not recognize the wisdom of God. Caiaphas, Herod and Pilate, under the influence of supernatural evil powers, were blind to what God was doing in Christ. Had they understood "they would not have crucified the Lord of glory" (v. 8). One time poet laureate, John Masefield, imagines Pilate's wife asking the centurion who carried out the crucifixion: "Do you think he's dead?" "No, lady, I don't." "Then where is he?" "Let loose in the world, lady, where neither Roman nor Jew can stop his truth."

## II. Revelation of Wisdom (2:9-12)

Those who are under the dominion of the present world-rulers do not have eyes to see the wisdom of God displayed at the cross. But for those who love him God has prepared "what no eye has seen, nor ear heard, nor the heart of man conceived" (v. 9). It is as Blaise Pascal put it: "Divine things to be known have to be loved."

The language of verse 9 comes from an unknown literary source, although Paul introduces the quotation as if it were an OT passage ("as it is written"). Origen thought Paul was quoting from the Apocalypse of Elijah. The Gospel of Thomas (17) ascribes these words to Jesus. Since footnoting was not practiced by ancient writers the source of Paul's quotation remains unknown. The language of the quotation bears some similarities to OT phraseology.

Although the things "which God has prepared" for us are not fully visible as long as we are in this life, we are given a foretaste of future glory by the Spirit of God. To "us" (who love God), Paul explains, God has revealed the wonderful mysteries of his plan of redemption, which the unbelieving world considers foolishness. And since God's revelation came to us as a gracious gift, we can take no credit for it. Unfortunately, humility has not always characterized those who had a good grasp of divine truth. Were it not for the Holy Spirit, who searches "even the depths of God" (v. 10), we would be as blind as pagan society around us.

By way of comparison, Paul goes on to say, no one knows a person's thoughts except the spirit of the person in him (v. 11). Whatever lie-detectors and psychoanalysts may dig out of a person, in the final analysis only we know our own thoughts (that God knows us even better, is thereby not denied). Similarly, only the Spirit of God knows what is in God and therefore, only he can reveal God's will for mankind to us.

Believers, as distinct from those who are informed by the spirit of the world, have received the Spirit of God. As a result, they are able to understand "the gifts bestowed on us by God" (v. 12). Not only, then, is the Spirit the agent of all revelation from God, but he also enlightens our minds so that we can grasp this revelation.

We should not overlook the significance of meditation, research and hard work in our effort to grasp what God has revealed to us in Jesus Christ. The Holy Spirit, for example, will not teach us Hebrew and Greek. Even Luke, the inspired writer, admits that he did a lot of research before writing his gospel (Lk. 1:1ff.). But, while any historian may discover from secular sources that Jesus was crucified under Pontius Pilate, he needs the illumination of the Spirit to understand that he died for our sins. And that makes a world of difference.

### III. Communication of Divine Wisdom (2:13)

The Spirit not only reveals God's truth and enlightens our minds to grasp it, he also comes to our aid in speaking about spiritual things. "And we impart this in words not taught by human wisdom but taught by the Spirit, interpreting spiritual truths to those who possess the Spirit" (v. 13).

The translation of the last line of this verse is very problematic. It could mean "interpreting spiritual truths for spiritual people," "interpreting spiritual truths by spiritual truths," "comparing spiritual truths with spiritual truths," and so forth. The first part of the verse makes it clear, however, that we need more than human expertise to communicate divine truths. A good command of the English language does not guarantee the communication of divine truth to English-speaking hearers. Not that the Spirit teaches us to use a special kind of religious vocabulary. In fact, to convey the Good News to modern man the Spirit may force us to rid ourselves of some of our religious jargon that our contemporaries do not understand.

John R.W. Stott warns us against drawing unwarranted conclusions from dependence on the Holy Spirit. "Trust in the Holy Spirit is not intended to save us the bother of preparation. The Holy Spirit can indeed give us utterance if we are suddenly called upon to speak and there has been no opportunity to prepare. But he can also clarify and direct our thinking in our study. Indeed, experience suggests that he does a better job there than in the pulpit" ( Christian Mission, p. 126).

But there is a level of communication which transcends the linguistic level. Without the help of the Spirit all our beautiful words sound hollow and fall to the ground.

### IV. Perception of Divine Wisdom (2:14-3:4)

(a) *By unbelievers* (v. 14). It is precisely because the "natural man" does not receive the things of the Spirit of God that we need the Spirit's help in communicating spiritual truths.

It is hard to know how to translate the word *psychikos* — "soulish," "psychical," "physical," "sensual," "natural"? It is the person who does not have the Spirit of God, the unbeliever, the unspiritual person, in contrast to the believer who has God's Spirit and who is therefore spiritual.

The unbeliever lacks, as it were, the proper antenna to receive the waves of eternity. He may have a brilliant intellect, he may be extremely knowledgeable in earthly matters (science, economics, politics, the arts), but because he lacks God's Spirit, he cannot appreciate God's revelation. He may be highly educated, but his horizons are too small to include the gospel of salvation. Indeed the gospel is folly to him, for it is understood only by the help of the Spirit of God, and this help is not available to fallen man as long as he rejects God's saving grace.

(b) *By the spiritual* (vv. 15,16). Whereas the unbeliever lacks the ability to perceive what God has done in Christ, he who has the Spirit of God has the equipment to discern God's truth. He has "Christ's mind" by which he is instructed.

When Paul says that such a person "judges all things" he does not mean that he knows more about economics or politics than an unbeliever (although even in such fields he can often look more deeply because of his knowledge of God and human nature), but he has the ability to grasp spiritual things. Or, to put it differently, he looks at all of life from a different vantage point.

Certainly Paul does not mean that the believer is above criticism, when he says that he is "judged by no one" (v. 15), but to the unbeliever he remains an enigma. Moreover, in the final analysis it is God (not man) who will judge him. In any case he cannot be assessed by those who do not have the Spirit of God.

(c) *By the immature* (3:1-4). Whereas all believers have the Spirit of God and, consequently, have the ability to understand God's revelation, some Christians are so immature that they never get past the abc's of the gospel. When Paul was in Corinth the first time his converts were obviously just "babes" in Christ and, as a wise master teacher, the apostle fed them only milk, not solids. But, as C.S. Lewis wrote in *Mere Christianity,* one can't go on indefinitely being an ordinary, decent egg. We must be hatched or go bad.

What distresses Paul, as he writes, is the fact that they never seem to have got out of their baby-shoes. "You still aren't able," is his poignant observation. The reason, however, is not age, but attitude. Where people are jealous and quarrel over leaders they don't behave as spiritual people should, and so there is a third category: the carnal, fleshly, worldly Christians. On the other hand, when they behave in a fleshly manner, "they are merely men" — just ordinary people who do not have Christ's Spirit.

And so, after a long detour, we are back at the problem of party-strife in Corinth which Paul is seeking to overcome. As we think of ourselves, is it not true that we who have the Spirit of God only too often live like ordinary people?

That kind of life will not attract others.

### Personal Response

1. *Define "worldly wisdom" and "godly wisdom" (vv. 2:6-7). Make a list of characteristics of each. How are they different? Are there any ways in which they are alike? How?*
2. *How do believers attain godly wisdom (vv. 2:9-16)? Share experiences of how God has revealed his wisdom to you.*
3. *What is the value of education? What added dimension does godly wisdom bring to education?*
4. *How can we help each other become more mature in godly wisdom?*
5. *How does our base of knowledge affect our conduct?*

# CHAPTER FIVE

## Paul Looks at Servanthood

*What, after all, is Apollos? And what is Paul? Only servants, through whom you came to believe — as the Lord has assigned to each his task. I planted the seed, Apollos watered it, but God made it grow. So neither he who plants nor he who waters is anything, but only God, who makes things grow. The man who plants and the man who waters have one purpose, and each will be rewarded according to his own labor. For we are God's fellow workers; you are God's field, God's building.*

*By the grace God has given me, I laid a foundation as an expert builder, and someone else is building on it. But each one should be careful how he builds. For no one can lay any foundation other than the one already laid, which is Jesus Christ. If any man builds on this foundation using gold, silver, costly stones, word, hay or straw, his work will be shown for what it is, because the Day will bring it to light. It will be revealed with fire, and the fire will test the quality of each man's work. If what he has built survives, he will receive his reward. If it is burned up, he will suffer loss; he himself will be saved, but only as one escaping through the flames.*

*Don't you know that you yourselves are God's temple and that God's Spirit lives in you? If anyone destroys God's temple, God will destroy him; for God's temple is sacred, and you are that temple.*

*Do not deceive yourselves. If any one of you thinks he is wise by the standards of this age, he should become a "fool" so that he*

29

*may become wise. For the wisdom of this world is foolishness in
God's sight. As it is written: "He catches the wise in their craftiness"; and again, "The Lord knows that the thoughts of the wise
are futile." So then, no more boasting about men! All things are
yours, whether Paul or Apollos or Cephas or the world or life or
death or the present or the future — all are yours, and you are of
Christ, and Christ is of God (I Corinthians 3:5-23).*

Members of the Corinthian church were asking: "Who is the
greatest among our leaders?"

The question stemmed from a worldly mind-set, for Jesus had
taught that true greatness in the kingdom of God is seen in servanthood (Lk. 22:24-27). To overcome this very human way of looking
at leadership in the church Paul gave his readers a long discourse
in divine versus human wisdom.

It is the apostle's hope that the Corinthians will learn to look
at the ministry from a higher vantage point, and consequently,
desist from rallying around their favorite teachers and preachers.

Paul's perspectives on service in the kingdom of God must be
taken seriously by the church in every age.

## I. Diversity Among God's Servants (3:5-9)

Our passage begins with several rhetorical questions: "What is
Apollos? What is Paul?" They knew "who" these men were, but
Paul wasn't sure the readers had recognized "what" they were. His
answer is: *diakonoi* (servants)! The word originally meant a table-
waiter. Then it came to be used for servants generally, and finally,
it is the word "deacon." In our passage it is used to stress the
lowliness of the preachers and teachers. If they are all servants,
then the attempt to rank them seems rather ridiculous.

This is underscored further by the explanation that each servant carries out his ministry "as the Lord assigned to each" (v. 5).
And if God equips his servants in different ways so that they can
fulfill their assigned duties, then why should one be pitted against
the other? No one can really take the other's place; no one works
in exactly the same manner as the other.

When Ned Stonehouse was asked to fill the vacancy left by the
death of Gresham Machen, professor of New Testament at
Westminster Theological Seminary, he made it clear in his inaugural ad-
dress that he could only "succeed" Dr. Machen, not "replace" him. God

in his infinite wisdom has made us all different, and so we may as well accept that and spare ourselves the trouble of trying to be someone else.

With the use of an agricultural metaphor that is easily understood even by city dwellers, Paul illustrates the diversity in the service of God. "I planted, Apollos watered, but God gave the growth" (v. 6). Why Cephas is not mentioned is not known; he may never have ministered in Corinth.

Paul was called to plant churches. He never stayed on as pastor. That he left to others. Paul travelled all over the Mediterranean world establishing light-centers; and while he was always ready to counsel and instruct, he let others water his plantings. The pastors who faithfully nurtured his converts after he left were not his rivals but his partners. "He who plants and he who waters are one" (v. 8). They work on the same field and both recognize that unless God makes the plants grow, all of God's servants labor in vain. "So neither he who plants nor he who waters is anything, but only God who gives the growth" (v. 7).

That does not mean, however, that their labors are not valued by God. To the contrary, "each shall receive his wages according to his labor" (v. 8). This should offset the possible misunderstanding that it makes no difference how we do our work on God's field. God rewards us according to our labors. The word *kopos* (labor) means hard, exhaustive work. It was a term used to describe missionary activity in the early church (cf. I Thess. 1:3; 2:9).

Having reduced the preachers and teachers of the church to the level of servanthood, Paul turns right around and exalts them beyond all measure: "We are God's fellow-workers." One could read the compound noun *synergoi* (fellow-workers) as "workers together for God" (RSV) or, as "God's fellow-workers" (NEB). While the latter is a daring claim, it is possible that Paul meant to say that we work together with God on his field. This should not give us a God-complex, but it should free us from those paralyzing feelings of worthlessness which creep over God's servants from time to time.

From the picture of the church as God's tilled field (*georgion* in Greek; *georgos* — our "George" — means "farmer") Paul switches to an architectural image, namely that of a building under construction. This leads him to expand on the theme of final judgment, when the labor of God's servants will be tested.

## II. The Testing (3:10-15)

Paul was equipped by God's grace to lay the foundation of the Corinthian church. He calls himself a "wise architect" (v. 10). Others are now the church's teachers and they build on the foundation he laid. His concern is that they build carefully.

The apostle recognizes, of course, that "no other foundation can any one lay than that which is laid, which is Jesus Christ" (v. 11 — Menno Simons' favorite text). Ultimately the church has its origin in Christ; however, he used Peter and other apostles to establish his church, and so the church can also be said to be "built upon the foundation of the apostles and prophets" (Eph. 2:20).

Paul had planted the church at Corinth; others now built on this foundation. The materials they used in the building were either combustible or non-combustible. Gold, silver and precious stones can stand a fire; wood, hay and stubble go up in flames. (It is this imagery that gave Luther the silly notion to call the Epistle of James a "strawy" epistle, since in his view it was poor building material.)

Precisely what Paul had in mind when he distinguished between durable and inflammable building materials is not stated. Certainly false teaching is not good building material.

An old man lay dying, troubled in conscience. As a boy he had turned a road-sign around making the arrow point the wrong way. It was a boyish prank but it bothered him to think that he may have misled many a traveller. False teaching can lead others astray. A frightening thought!

However, we should include also the methods by which we build, when we think of building materials. These, too, must be in the spirit of Jesus. After all, Jesus is not simply a landmark beside which we can exercise our "free masonry." Perhaps even the members of the church themselves should be included. If they are not "living stones" the building will not pass the fire test.

This test comes at the last day. "The Day will disclose it" (v. 13). The *Day* is shorthand for "the Day of the Lord," the second coming of Christ, the *parousia*. This day will be a glorious day for the saints, but it will also be a day when our life-work is judged. This *Day* "will be revealed in fire." Fire is a symbol of judgment, often found in OT descriptions of the "Day of the Lord" (Joel 2:3; Mal. 4:1).

On this day of judgment our works will be examined: what we

did, how we did it, why we did it. "If the work of someone remains...he shall receive wages" (v. 14). No doubt there will be many surprises on that day. How shattering if much of our life's work should go up in smoke!

"If any man's work is burned up, he will suffer loss, though he himself will be saved, but only as through fire" (v. 15). The picture is that of a burning building from which a person escapes by the skin of his teeth; loses everything except his life. What is at stake, then, is not our salvation, but our reward. Let us, therefore, work for our Lord humbly and honestly so that we do "not lose what (we) have worked for, but win a full wage" (II Jn. 8).

Since God will do the final testing of his servants, the Corinthians may as well leave that to him and desist from passing judgment on their leaders. Much rather should they learn to appreciate all of them.

### III. Appreciation of God's Servants (3:16-23)

It was the hope of the prophets that God's temple would be restored in the age to come. This hope was fulfilled, in part at least, in the church, the temple of the Spirit. If God dwells among his people by the Holy Spirit, then one ought to think twice before one undermines this temple. "If anyone destroys God's temple, God will destroy him" (v. 17). Sins against the Jerusalem temple were taken very seriously in Judaism. Stephen was stoned for speaking against the temple. Sins against the church are no less serious.

Paul probably has the tearing up of the church through party-strife in mind, and warns his readers against such violations of the sanctity of the temple of the Spirit, the church. And so the Corinthians better beware and not be too worldly wise and conceited (v. 18). With a quote from Job 5:13 (the only other quote from Job in the New Testament is Rom. 11:35). Pauls reminds his readers that God traps arrogant people in their craftiness (v. 19). A passage from Psalm 94:11 underscores this warning: "The Lord knows that the thoughts of the wise are futile" (v. 20).

The apostle explained in chapters 1 and 2 that worldly wisdom had made his converts contentious. They were fighting over their leaders; applying worldly standards. Paul exhorts them to stop boasting in men (v. 21). There is a legitimate pride that people can have in their teachers, or their pastor; however, by pitting one preacher against another people impoverish themselves. Paul, Apollos and Cephas all belonged to the Corinthians. Of course, some people will prefer to hear Paul rather than Apollos, and vice versa, but that does not mean that the other should not be respected for the contribution he makes to the church in his own way.

Having begun to describe the wealth which the church has in its teachers and preachers, Paul concludes with a lyrical outburst. Not only do the ministers belong to the church, but the world and life and death, the present and future as well (v. 22). Because we belong to Christ, who belongs to God (v. 23), all the riches of God are ours. To be sure, we have but a foretaste of these riches here in this life, but "if we are children, then heirs, heirs of God and fellow heirs of Christ" (Rom. 8:17).

### *Personal Response*

1. *The Corinthian people were causing divisions in the church by following certain leaders (v. 5). How do believers cause division in the church today?*
2. *Think of people who were/are influential in your life. What contribution did/does each make?*
3. *How can we show appreciation for people who are influential in our lives (v. 8)?*
4. *Describe the differences between a "servant" leader and a "ruler" leader (vv. 5-9).*
5. *Think about the activities which are important in your individual life and in your church (vv. 10-15). Which ones are of perishable materials? Which are of permanent materials?*

# CHAPTER SIX

## Ministers of the Gospel

*So then, men ought to regard us as servants of Christ and as those entrusted with the secret things of God. Now it is required that those who have been given a trust must prove faithful. I care very little if I am judged by you or by any human court; indeed, I do not even judge myself. My conscience is clear, but that does not make me innocent. It is the Lord who judges me. Therefore judge nothing before the appointed time; wait till the Lord comes. He will bring to light what is hidden in darkness and will expose the motives of men's hearts. At that time each will receive his praise from God.*

*Now, brothers, I have applied these things to myself and Apollos for your benefit, so that you may learn from us the meaning of the saying, "Do not go beyond what is written." Then you will not take pride in one man over against another. For who makes you different from anyone else? What do you have that you did not receive? And if you did receive it, why do you boast as though you did not?*

*Already you have all you want! Already you have become rich! You have become kings — and that without us! How? I wish that you really had become kings so that we might be kings with you! For it seems to me that God has put us apostles on display at the end of the procession, like men condemned to die in the arena. We have been made a spectacle to the whole universe, to angels as well as to men. We are fools for Christ, but you are so wise in Christ! We*

*are weak, but you are strong! You are honored, we are dishonored!*
*To this very hour we go hungry and thirsty, we are in rags, we are*
*brutally treated, we are homeless. We work hard with our own*
*hands. When we are cursed, we bless; when we are persecuted, we*
*endure it; when we are slandered, we answer kindly. Up to this mo-*
*ment we have become the scum of the earth, the refuse of the world.*

*I am not writing this to shame you, but to warn you, as my dear*
*children. Even though you have ten thousand guardians in Christ,*
*you do not have many fathers, for in Christ Jesus I became your*
*father through the gospel. Therefore I urge you to imitate me. For*
*this reason I am sending to you Timothy, my son whom I love, who*
*is faithful in the Lord. He will remind you of my way of life in Christ*
*Jesus, which agrees with what I teach everywhere in every church.*

*Some of you have become arrogant, as if I were not coming to*
*you. But I will come to you very soon, if the Lord is willing, and then*
*I will find out not only how these arrogant people are talking, but*
*what power they have. For the kingdom of God is not a matter of*
*talk but of power. What do you prefer? Shall I come to you with a*
*whip, or in love and with a gentle spirit? (I Corinthians 4:1-21).*

The word "minister" in its earlier usage meant "servant," and
that is how our topic is to be understood. Our chapter focuses on
those who are called to preach the gospel and to instruct the church
in the ways of God. The question Paul raises is: How shall churches
look at the ministers of the gospel?

His first answer is: "as servants" (v. 1). Had the Corinthians
thought of Paul, Apollos and others in this way they would not
have quarrelled so fiercely over which of their leaders was the
greatest.

To be a servant of the church does not mean, however, that the
church should look upon itself as the lord over its ministers (or,
what is worse, their employer). There is, after all, another side to
the ministry. Ministers are also "stewards of the mysteries of God"
(v. 1). The word "steward" (*oikonomos*) is taken from the socioeconomic world of Paul, and meant, to begin with, the manager of
a household. Eventually it was used for any kind of manager of someone else's property.

The "mysteries of God" are God's revelation. The word
"mystery" suggests that we cannot know God's saving plans unless
he makes them known to us, and so they remain hidden in God until he removes the veil. This he has done in Jesus Christ, and now

we as God's ministers are to proclaim, to teach, to guard these sacred truths which God has given his church, recorded for us in the apostolic writings. And, as in ordinary life, so in the ministry, the supreme requirement for stewardship is faithfulness (v. 2).

We have not been called to proclaim our own ideas, dreams or visions, but to teach faithfully the word of God. Menno Simons wrote: "Brethren...I am not Enoch, I am not Elijah, I am not one who sees visions, I am not a prophet who can teach and prophesy, otherwise than what is written in the Word of God and understood in the Spirit."

As servants of God and stewards of God's mysteries the ministers of the gospel work in the public eye and, consequently, are evaluated, criticized and praised. Let us see what Paul has to say about the evaluation of ministers!

### I. Evaluation of God's Ministers (4:1-5)

When the author graduated from seminary in 1953, the president alerted us to the fact that we were now leaving the ranks of the critics and joining the ranks of the criticized. No one serving the public can escape criticism, and Luther suggested that one of the requirements for the ministry is the willingness to be flayed by everyone.

For Paul, however, "it was a small thing to be judged" by the Corinthians or "by any human court" (v. 3). He is not slighting courts of law but the judgment "days" in Corinth, where he was compared with other leaders and given only a passing grade by some of his converts. Not that Paul disregards the opinions of others; he is very concerned to have the goodwill of people. But he will not let a bit of criticism blow him off the field or a bit of praise puff him up.

Whereas Paul will not allow the criticism of others to crush him, there is one critic who is with Paul all the time: his conscience. From the pastoral epistles we learn how important a good conscience is. Here, however, we discover that even a good conscience cannot be the final judge of our ministry. "I am not aware of anything against myself, but I am not thereby acquitted" (v. 4).

Conscience always functions in accordance with the light we have. Terrible things have been done with a good conscience. Indeed, Paul had persecuted the church with a good conscience, but in blindness. Conscience may congratulate us on our ministry, or it may condemn us. Conscience, however, does not have the final word to say. Who then does? "It is the Lord who judges me."

It would be unwise to dismiss the evaluations of our brothers as inconsequential. Also, one cannot continue to minister with a guilt-ridden conscience. However, the last word about our ministry will be spoken by God on the last day.

God is called the *kardiognostes* in the Bible (Acts 1:24) — the heart specialist, the heart-examiner — and he penetrates to the very core of our being and knows "the hidden purposes of the heart" (v. 5). On the last day our motives, our accomplishments, our failures, everything will be brought to light. And lest we fear that nothing we have done will pass God's fire-test, Paul assures us that on the last day "every person will receive his commendation from God" (v. 5).

Since the work of every minister will be weighed in God's balances on that day, it is highly inappropriate for any one to pass final judgment on the work of a minister of the gospel. We make our evaluations, we may even criticize, but we dare not speak the last word on any person's ministry.

## II. The Lowliness of God's Ministers (4:6-13)

Divisions over spiritual leaders in Corinth stemmed from an evil root, namely, pride. Using himself and his co-workers as examples, Paul will show the Corinthians how humbly God's servants live. He hopes that the lowliness of the apostles will prick the bubble of pride so "that none of you may be puffed up in favor of one against the other" (v. 6). Pride in their favorite leader had led to the denigration of other leaders.

With a series of rhetorical questions Paul hammers away at the pride of the Corinthians. "Who made you to differ?" (i.e., to get superior over the next person). "What do you have that you did not receive?" If God endows people differently by his grace, then why should one feel superior to the other. Helmut Thielicke told a bright young university student: "You are very gifted." The young fellow blushed with pride, and so Thielicke quickly added: "I did not say you were a good man; all I said was that you were gifted, and of course you have nothing to do with that." In the words of Paul: "If then you received it, why do you boast as if it were not a gift?" (v. 7).

Paul adds a touch of sarcasm to a series of rhetorical

affirmations. "Already you are filled! Already you have become rich! Without us you have become kings! And would you did so reign, so that we might share the rule with you"! (v. 8).

In contrast to the apostles who still had to suffer abuse, the Corinthians, in their spiritual pride, were living on dizzy heights. They acted as if they were already in the final kingdom. It was only a pity, Paul suggests, that the apostles couldn't live on cloud nine with them.

David Bosch tells of a book in which a well-known Christian writer promises his readers techniques by which they can gain self-confidence, vigor, success and spiritual healing. Included is a ten-point guide to popularity ( Spirituality of the Road, p. 81). Paul's life was one of weakness, affliction, and self-denial.

He pictures himself and his co-workers as doomed wretches on the way to the arena where they will die (v. 9). In contrast to the hyperspiritual Corinthians, who are wise, strong and held in honor, the apostles are weak, despised, looked upon as fools (v. 10). There must have been many red faces when this letter was read in the Corinthian congregation!

Like his Master, Paul suffers from hunger and thirst; he is often abused and has no fixed abode (v. 11). This homeless vagabond did not think it beneath his dignity to support himself with the work of his hands (v. 12). Like the Master, the apostles bless when reviled; endure persecution and slander. Indeed, they are treated like refuse, like the scum of society, the scapegoats of the community. What a scathing indictment of the luxurious life-style of some Christian leaders in our day!

### III. The Concern of God's Minister (4:14-21)

Having cautioned the Corinthians against a false evaluation of God's servants, and having pictured the ministers of the gospel in their earthly weakness and suffering, Paul finally brings his long discourse on the ministry to an end with some personal appeals.

By now the readers must have felt thoroughly ashamed and Paul explains that it was not his ultimate purpose to humiliate them, but to admonish them (v. 14). The word "admonish" (*noutheteo*) has several nuances. It means, on the one hand, to straighten someone out in his thinking; on the other, it means to make a tender appeal. If they weren't his "beloved children," Paul might let things ride, but since he's concerned about them, he admonishes them. For while they may have countless guides (*paidagogi*) in Christ, they have only one spiritual father. Through the gospel Paul had led them to Christ (v. 15). And, since it is only natural that children resemble their father, the apostle calls on his children to imitate him (v. 16). The example of Christian leaders was much more crucial in the early period of the Christian church, when believers did not yet have the New Testament writings. But even today, there is nothing quite so inspiring as a human model that calls for imitation.

In order to put the Corinthians back on track, Paul has sent his faithful legate, Timothy, to remind them of his "ways in Christ" (v. 17). Paul's "ways" are his teachings, which lead to a new way of life. Christians were known as "people of the way." To be a Christian does not simply mean to believe certain things, but to live in a certain way.

They knew what Paul taught, but they needed to be "reminded." The author had a room mate at Wheaton College who never went to church on Sundays because, as he explained, he never heard anything new there. But we need to be "reminded" of what we know. Our practice usually lags far behind our knowledge. Abraham H. Unruh used to say that the forgetfullness of his hearers gave him courage to keep on preaching.

Some Corinthians were sure that Paul was too timid to return to Corinth, but Paul assures them that he will come "if the Lord wills" (vv. 18,19). Paul made plans, but often his plans went awry, and so he had learned to live in submission to God. In earlier days Christians often wrote D.V. after their plans (*deo volente*, "the Lord willing"). Whether we write it or not, it should always be in our minds when we make our plans.

If Paul, in God's providence, should come to them, he will pay little attention to the spiritual boasting of the high-octane Corinthians. He wants to see God's power at work in their lives (v. 19), for that's a more trustworthy criterion of whether God's kingdom is present in their midst (v. 20). Their response to Paul's letter and to Timothy's visit will determine whether Paul will come "with a rod," to chastise them, or whether he will come "with love in a spirit of gentleness" (v. 21).

With that Paul concludes his discourse on the first topic of this letter: party strife. He will now turn to the problem of immorality litigation and permissiveness. Let us continue to listen to him!

## Personal Response

1. What changes in attitudes have accompanied the movement from lay ministers in the church to paid pastors *(vv. 1-5)*?
2. What criteria do we use to judge pastors today *(vv. 6-7)*? Are they biblical criteria?
3. What is the role of pastors and lay persons in the church?
4. How can parishioners and pastors work together to further the ministries of the church?
5. What is the relationship between lay persons and pastors within the church *(vv. 14-17)*?

# CHAPTER SEVEN

## Paul Teaches Church Discipline

*It is actually reported that there is sexual immorality among you, and of a kind that does not occur even among pagans: A man has his father's wife. And you are proud! Shouldn't you rather have been filled with grief and have put out of your fellowship the man who did this? Even though I am not physically present, I am with you in spirit. And I have already passed judgment on the one who did this, just as if I were present. When you are assembled in the name of our Lord Jesus and I am with you in spirit, and the power of our Lord Jesus is present, hand this man over to Satan, so that the sinful nature may be destroyed and his spirit saved on the day of the lord.*

*Your boasting is not good. Don't you know that a little yeast works through the whole batch of dough. Get rid of the old yeast that you may be a new batch without yeast — as you really are. For Christ, our Passover Lamb, has been sacrificed. Therefore let us keep the Festival, not with the old yeast, the yeast of malice and wickedness, but with bread without yeast, the bread of sincerity and truth.*

*I have written you in my letter not to associate with sexually immoral people — not at all meaning the people of this world who are immoral, or the greedy and swindlers, or idolaters. In that case you would have to leave this world. But now I am writing you that you must not associate with anyone who calls himself a brother but is sexually immoral or greedy, an idolater or a slanderer, a drunkard*

*or a swindler. With such a man do not even eat.*
*What business is it of mine to judge those outside the church?*
*Are you not to judge those inside? God will judge those outside. "Ex-*
*pel the wicked man from among you" (I Corinthians 5:1-13).*

It is possible that Paul was about to conclude his letter to the
Corinthians when further news from Corinth arrived. The apostle
had already dispatched Timothy to Corinth, in the hope that he
would help the church overcome some of its difficulties. Paul also
had in mind to visit them. Since, however, the time of his coming
was still indefinite, he continued to instruct his converts by letter.

This highly gifted congregation was plagued by carnality.
Worldly wisdom not only caused party-strife, but it also led the
Corinthians to the most blatant disregard of some basic concepts of
Christian morality. Although they had the gift of the Spirit, many
of the members of the Corinthian church behaved, as Paul said,
like "ordinary men" (3:3).

In spite of a case of gross immorality in the church, the Corinthians had done nothing about it. Paul castigates them for the total
neglect of church discipline.

## I. Failure of the Corinthians (5:1,2)

The chapter begins abruptly — suggesting that Paul is shocked
at what he has heard. Fornication (Greek: *porneia)* was practiced by
a member of the church and the church winked at it. It was the sort
of thing that even pagan taboos condemned: a man was living with
his father's wife.

Whether the woman was a church member is not known, but
the man was. The woman is not the offender's mother, but possibly
his step-mother. Whether her husband was dead or divorced is not
known. Paul doesn't need to inform the Corinthians on such sordid
details; they know the situation. It was a case of incest, condemned
by the Torah as well as by Roman law.

What is even more shocking to Paul is the fact that his readers
were "puffed up," arrogant in the light of such monstrous violations of Christian standards. It may be that they had carried the
concept of Christian liberty, freedom from the law, to ridiculous extremes. In any case, they did not feel particularly sad about the
situation. Had the church mourned when such a gross evil came to

light, they would have inaugurated disciplinary action.

In our reaction to the harsh discipline practiced at times by our churches in the past, we stand in great danger today of falling into the Corinthian error of doing nothing, even when serious lapses in Christian behavior occur. To be loving, accepting and forgiving does not mean that we allow evil to flourish unchecked in the ranks of the believing community.

## II. Discipline of the Offender (5:3-5)

Since the Corinthians had not done anything about this failure in morality, Paul now tells the church what they ought to do. (One should notice that it's the "church," not simply the leaders, who are to act.)

The Corinthians must call a meeting of the congregation. Paul will be with them in spirit, and then they are to act in keeping with the apostle's decision: to deliver this man over to Satan. The translation of verses 3 and 4 is problematic, but the following inferences can be legitimately made:

First, when the church gathers it does so in Jesus' name. And that means also that Jesus' power is at work in the congregation. The church is more than a social club. Christ is present when his people gather.

Second, the gathered community is to give the offender over to Satan. That means excommunication from the church. Outside the church is the realm of Satan and to be expelled from the church is to be transferred to that realm. "For the destruction of the flesh" seems to go beyond expulsion from the church. The view that "flesh" refers to the man's fleshly way of life, which is to be corrected through discipline, does not seem to fit the context very well. More likely physical suffering is meant.

If Job, who was innocent, was given over to Satan for the affliction of his flesh (Job 2:5), how much more might one who had polluted the temple of God (I Cor. 3:17) be exposed to sickness and death. Should this be the correct meaning, then it would appear as if we have a situation here not unlike that of Ananias and Sapphira. We who are not apostles should probably not go that far in our discipline. "This was an extreme exercise of the apostolic authority of binding and loosing; we should not dare to do anything of the kind" (F.F. Bruce, *Answers*, p. 91).

Third, regardless of how severe the discipline, the church must always act with the hope that the offender will be saved. "That his spirit may be saved in the day of the Lord Jesus" (v. 5). Paul's hope evidently was that discipline by the church would lead the offender to repentance and, even if he should die, that he would be among the redeemed on the day of judgment.

### III. The Admonition by the Apostle (5:6-8)

Leaving the particular case of discipline aside for a moment, Paul explains that when such tragedies occur in the church, boasting is sorely out of place. Rather than boast in their tolerance, they should have humbled themselves before God.

When a church winks at evil in the life of one of its members there is always a danger that the entire body be infected. "A little leaven leavens the whole lump" (v. 6). Leaven was left-over dough, used for yeast, and is used here as a metaphor for the pervasive power of evil. (In the Parable of the Leaven, Mt. 13:33, it is used in a positive sense for the growth of the kingdom.) It was a proverbial saying, meaning that little causes can have grave consequences.

It may be that Paul wrote this letter during Passover, when Jewish homes were cleansed of leaven in anticipation of the Feast of Unleavened Bread, which began with Passover. With candles in hand, every corner of the house was searched for crumbs of leavened bread. Nowadays the head of the Jewish household simply declares the house to be free of leaven. (It has been suggested that the Western housewives got the notion of spring cleaning from this Jewish custom.)

And so Paul exhorts the church to "cleanse out the old leaven that you may be a new lump, as you really are unleavened" (v. 7). They had become a "fresh baking" in Christ and they were now to act in accord with the new beginning. The "old leaven" is a reference to the life of sin they left behind when they became a "new creation" in Christ. If then a member of the church persists in sin, such "leaven" has to be cleared out of the church. That the Corinthians were negligent in their "house-cleaning" is underscored by reminding them that "Christ, our paschal lamb, has been sacrificed." In Israel the house was cleansed before Passover; in Corinth Passover was past (Christ had died), but the house was still full of leaven. The readers are exhorted to celebrate the paschal festival, not for a week, as was Jewish custom, nor simply on Good Friday, as in later Christian practice, but every day of their life. How should they do this? By living lives that are free from the old leaven of malice and evil; lives characterized, rather, by sincerity and truth (v. 8).

## IV. Explanation of a Letter (5:9-13)

The failure of the Corinthians to overcome immorality in the ranks of the church seems to have reminded Paul of an earlier letter he wrote to them. In this letter he had warned them against associating with immoral people (literally, "don't get mixed up with fornicators," v. 9). Evidently some Corinthians had misconstrued this to mean that they should no longer associate with non-Christian people. How could one live in Corinth, a city which was proverbial for bad morals, and not associate with immoral people? One couldn't! In the words of Bunyan: "The way to the Celestial City lies through the town where this lusty fair is kept; and he that will go to the City, and yet not go through this town, must needs 'go out of the world'" (*The Pilgrim's Progress*, Part i).

Paul nowhere counsels Christians to leave the evil city and to withdraw from the world. He did not mean, as he explains, that they were to refrain from associating with the greedy, with robbers and with idolators. Christians do business with the ungodly; they may have pagan neighbors; their grocer may be an immoral person. How could Christians witness to Christ's love if they had no contact with people outside the Christian faith?

What Paul really meant in his former letter to the Corinthians (a letter that has been lost) was that Christians should not have fellowship with immoral people in the church. If someone claims to be a "brother" (i.e. a Christian) and is guilty of fornication, greed, idolatry, drunkenness or the like, he is to be denied Christian fellowship.

In the Orient eating together was always a mark of friendship, and Paul does not want church members to have fellowship with Christians who live in sin. Obviously this also implies that such offenders have no place at the Lord's Table. Where the family feeling is strong in a congregation, such a denial of friendship, when done in the right spirit, normally leads to repentance and an acceptance back into fellowship.

The discipline of the church extends to its own members only. "For what have I to do with judging outsiders?" (v. 12). That does not mean that Christians should not feel indignant at society's evils, or that they should not exercise their "lifting power" in an evil world, but it means that the church does not have jurisdiction over the world. The power of binding and loosing (Mt. 18:18), of forgiving and retaining sins (Jn. 20:23) can be exercised only over "those inside the church."

That does not mean that God will let evil-doers get away with their sins. No, ultimately they must stand before the judge of all the earth. "God will judge those outside" (v. 13). With a quotation from Deuteronomy, Paul repeats that the church must assume responsibility for the discipline of its own members.

Obviously such instructions make good sense only in the context of the believers' church. It was in such a setting that Menno Simons wanted the "ban" to be practiced. No doubt he went too far in this, and many followers of Menno also went too far. But just as lying does not put the value of truthfulness in question, so the abuses of church discipline do not invalidate the teaching of the New Testament on this aspect of the church's life.

### Personal Response

1. *Paul was very clear on the necessity of church discipline (vv. 1-2, 9-11). Why are churches so hesitant to exercise church discipline?*
2. *What are some motivations for and results of church discipline (v. 5)?*
3. *How can Christians confront each other in loving ways? How can church discipline become redemptive?*
4. *How can believers have constructive, redemptive relationships with unbelievers?*

# CHAPTER EIGHT

## Christians and Lawsuits

*If any of you has a dispute with another, dare he take it before the ungodly for judgment instead of before the saints? Do you not know that the saints will judge the world? And if you are to judge the world, are you not competent to judge trivial cases? Do you not know that we will judge angels? How much more the things of this life! Therefore, if you have disputes about such matters, appoint as judges even men of little account in the church! I say this to shame you. Is it possible that there is nobody among you wise enough to judge a dispute between believers? But instead, one brother goes to law against another — and this in front of unbelievers!*

*The very fact that you have lawsuits among you means you have been completely defeated already. Why not rather be wronged? Why not rather be cheated? Instead, you yourselves cheat and do wrong, and you do this to your brothers.*

*Do you not know that the wicked will not inherit the kingdom of God? Do not be deceived: Neither the sexually immoral nor idolaters nor adulterers nor male prostitutes nor homosexual offenders nor thieves nor the greedy nor drunkards nor slanderers nor swindlers will inherit the kingdom of God. And that is what some of you were. But you were washed, you were sanctified, you were justified in the name of the Lord Jesus Christ and by the Spirit of our God (I Corinthians 6:1-11).*

49

In the previous chapter Paul explained that believers have no
jurisdiction over those outside the church. Conversely, he now cautions his readers against letting "outsiders" govern the life of the
church.

Evidently the Corinthians thought nothing of taking their
fellow-Christians to court to settle personal grievances, and the
mention of "judgment" in 5:12,13 led Paul to censure his converts
for such violations of Christian brotherhood. Our chapter opens
with a sharp rebuke.

## I. A Sharp Rebuke (6:1-8)

The apostle rebukes his readers, first, for settling their quarrels
in public (v. 1). He is shocked that a believer would take his brother
to court to settle a dispute (*pragma* in its legal sense is a cause for
trial, a case). "How does anyone dare?" he asks. The report that
some members of the Corinthian congregation were prosecuting
others, or suing for redress in civil courts came as a shock to Paul.

The Greeks loved litigation, and the Romans took pride in their
legal system which assured citizens all over the empire of justice
in court. Paul has no quarrel with the Roman legal system; he
himself enjoyed the protection that Roman law afforded. What he
cannot accept is that the church should wash its dirty linen in the
eyes of the world. Believers were suing each other for redress
"before the unrighteous." The "unrighteous" are not judges who
are partial or who bend the law; they are non-Christians,
unbelievers.

For a Jew like Paul such practice would be particularly
reprehensible, for Jews all over the Empire and beyond its frontiers
had their own machinery for the administration of justice within
the Jewish community. Pagans were not to arbitrate Jewish quarrels. If Jews did this, how much more should Christians hesitate to
settle grievances in public law court!

When Paul suggests that such grievances be settled "before the
saints," he does not mean that the entire congregation be involved
in every dispute between church members. Jesus outlined the pro-
cedure for such situations in Matthew 18:15-18. Nor is Paul suggesting that the church establish its own court system over against
the civil courts. But the church must settle its disputes within the
congregation, lest the gospel be brought into disrepute.

Paul rebukes his readers, also, for contradicting their high calling, by seeking redress in pagan courts (vv. 2,3). "Do you not know that the saints will judge the world? And if the world is to be judged by you, are you incompetent to try trivial cases?" (v. 2).

When Christ returns and this world is judged, believers will participate in this final judgment. Although this is nowhere explicitly stated in our gospels, Paul assumes that his readers are familiar with his teaching. It may be that this calling of the saints to judge the world was based on Daniel 7:22, where one like the Son of Man comes in glory and "judgment was given to the saints of the Most High."

That the saints, too, must stand before the judgment seat of Christ is not denied by Paul's statement. He does insist, however, that when Christ comes in glory and all the saints are united with him, they will have a part in the judgment of the world. Sometimes the word "judge" is used in the Hebraic sense of "reign," and that meaning should not be ruled out in our passage. That Christ's followers will sit on thrones and reign with him is stated at several places in the New Testament (e.g. Mt. 19:28; Rev. 20:4,5).

What seems even more staggering is Paul's claim that the saints shall some day judge angels (v. 3). Very likely evil angels are meant, for they are kept "in the nether gloom until the judgment of the great day" (Jude 6; II Peter 2:4). Also, angel-princes, who oppose God's emissaries today (Dan. 10:13,20), will in the end be judged, and the saints will participate in that judgment.

If the saints are called to such an exalted position, it is a downright shame when they cannot settle trivial cases here on earth. Of course, when there are grievances, these do not seem trivial to those involved. Indeed, they are usually blown out of all proportions. But in the light of the great day of judgment at the end of the age, earthly disputes are insignificant.

Paul rebukes the Corinthians, also, for a failure in brotherliness (vv. 4-8). If then a member of the church feels wronged by a fellow-believer, why go to court? "Why do you lay them (i.e. cases) before those who are least esteemed by the church?" (v. 4). Paul is not suggesting that pagan judges should not be respected, but that they have no status in the church; they have no place in church affairs. (It is hard to see how "the least esteemed" could refer to fellow church members.)

Since there is no punctuation in the early manuscripts one could read verse 4 as a statement rather than as a question. Moreover, the verb to "lay before" (*kathizete*) could be an imperative. In that event Paul is using irony. "Lay your cases before those who are least esteemed! Anyone can handle them!"

To their shame Paul asks whether there is no wise person among them who could arbitrate when quarrels between brothers arise (v. 5). That question must have stung in a congregation that was blessed with the gift of knowledge (1:5) and that prided itself on its wisdom. In contrast to the abundance of worldly wisdom in Corinth, there was a great paucity of true wisdom in the church — a wisdom that comes from above and which is peaceable.

To have to go to court is bad enough; to take a brother to court is even worse; to do so in the presence of unbelievers is worst of all (v. 6).

Several years ago, when driving by a church in Asuncion, I saw two soldiers with rifles in hand guarding the front entrance. When I inquired about this ghastly scene I was told that the congregation was split and each party was laying claim to the church property. Not a very inviting scene! It's a scene that is not uncommon in North American Christianity either — groups in the church suing the congregation, congregations suing the denomination, and the like.

To have lawsuits at all with fellow believers is a defeat (v. 7), says Paul. He does not mean that they will not be treated fairly by pagan judges, but even for the brother who wins his case in court such an experience is a defeat. It's a violation of Christian ethics. A legal victory may be a spiritual defeat.

We realize, of course, that lawsuits can be forced upon Christians. Moreover, there may be situations where the courts need to arbitrate in a situation where there are no personal grievances. But Christians should never go to public courts to get even with each other.

Jesus taught a "more excellent way." He spoke of turning the other cheek, of going the second mile. "If any one would sue you and take your coat, let him have your cloak as well" (Mt. 5:40). Paul is well aware of the way of Christ and admonishes his readers to permit themselves to be wronged and to be defrauded rather than to sue each other (v. 8). When Jesus was treated unjustly, he did not demand redress or vengeance. But in Corinth one brother was mistreating and defrauding the other. (The word "brother" occurs over and over again in this passage, to underscore the seriousness of the failure in Christian love.)

A good many years ago, as a member of the church council of my home church, we worked through a situation in which one member of the church had laid official charges against another who apparently had caused him some property damage. (The brothers are in glory today and so they won't be offended.) When this was discovered several brothers were delegated to plead with the accuser to withdraw his charges, and to his credit he did. Uppermost in the discussion (aside from the effort to bring the two brothers together again) was the concern that the church's good name in the community would not be besmirched and thereby Christ's name be dishonored.

Paul repeatedly admonishes the readers of his letters to live with care in the eyes of the outsiders. In our day where everyone insists on his "rights," Christians need to relearn what it means to suffer "wrongs."

## II. Warning to All Believers (6:9-11)

With the Corinthians still in his mind, Paul now issues a serious warning to all believers that unrighteous people will not inherit the kingdom of God (v. 9). The Corinthians, of course, knew this, but did not apply this knowledge to the matter of lawsuits.

This warning is addressed not to the wicked people of this world, but to believers. And the warnings of the Bible are not mere teasers; they warn against real dangers. To inherit the kingdom means to enter the eternal kingdom when Christ comes.

And lest there be any doubt about who the "unrighteous" are, Paul gives a long list of vices: fornicators, idolators, adulterers, homosexuals, thieves, greedy, drunkards, revilers, robbers (v. 10). The list is not exhaustive but is representative.

Tactfully Paul reminds his readers that "some of them" used to live in these sins but, of course, they had said farewell to such vices. Not that every Corinthian had indulged in all these black sins, nor that as Christians they may not in a weak moment fall into sin, but they got themselves washed (the middle voice in Greek stresses personal responsibility), they were sanctified, they were justified (v. 11).

The "washing" no doubt refers to their baptism; but water baptism signifies, among other things, that inner cleansing which only the Spirit of God can effect. Paul probably chose the verb "washed" or "baptized" because of the emphasis on cleansing from sin. They were washed clean on the basis of the finished work of Christ on the cross, and so their initiation is said to have taken place "in the name of the Lord Jesus Christ and by the Spirit of our God."

Since justification, sanctification and baptism were all part of the conversion experience in the early church, Paul can put them in whatever order he wishes. Justification, sanctification and baptism call the believer to pursue holiness "without which no one will see God" (Heb. 12:14).

### Personal Response

1. Paul indicates that believers should not be litigants against each other. What other models might the church use to settle disputes between believers (vv. 4-6)?
2. Why should unbelievers not judge disputes between believers (vv. 5-6)? (You may want to think beyond the text on this question.)
3. When is it proper to suffer "wrong" than be judged "right" (vv. 7-8)?
4. The primary stance of the court system is adversarial; one party is pitted against another. How can this be reconciled with the teaching of Jesus regarding love and reconciliation?
5. Today the interpretation of the law may vary with different judges, attorneys, juries, and litigants. Given the varying interpretations, are there instances when believers may need to have the courts decide the interpretation? What, if any, might these be?

# CHAPTER NINE

## Liberty or License?

*"Everything is permissible for me" — but not everything is beneficial. "Everything is permissible for me" — but I will not be mastered by anything. "Food for the stomach and the stomach for food" — but God will destroy them both. The body is not meant for sexual immorality, but for the Lord, and the Lord for the body. By his power God raised the Lord from the dead, and he will raise us also. Do you not know that your bodies are members of Christ himself? Shall I then take the members of Christ and unite them with a prostitute? Never! Do you not know that he who unites himself with a prostitute is one with her in body? For it is said, "The two will become one flesh." But he who unites himself with the Lord is one with him in spirit.*

*Flee from sexual immorality. All other sins a man commits are outside his body, but he who sins sexually sins against his own body. Do you not know that your body is a temple of the Holy Spirit, who is in you, whom you have received from God? You are not your own; you were bought at a price. Therefore honor God with your body (I Corinthians 6:12-20).*

Fornication was condoned by the average Greek and Roman alike. It was an integral part of pagan religion in Corinth. Converts to the Christian faith faced temptations on all sides to fall back into their former sinful ways.

This temptation was all the greater because the gospel of freedom, which Paul had preached, was evidently misconstrued by some Corinthians to mean license. And so, after dealing with a particularly obnoxious case of sexual immorality in chapter 5, Paul now zeroes in on the sin of fornication. He begins by correcting false notions of Christian liberty.

## I. Limitations of Christian Liberty (6:12)

"All things are lawful," seems to have been a current slogan in Corinth. Gnostic influence evidently made some Corinthians impatient of the restraints of conventional morality; they advocated the freedom to express one's desires.

In quoting this slogan Paul does not necessarily endorse it wholesale. In fact, he qualifies the watchword in two ways: (a) All things are lawful, but not all things are helpful." The word *symphero* ("helpful") means to "bear together" and so comes to mean "to profit."

There are many things in life which in themselves are neither good nor bad; they are neutral. But when they absorb our time and energy and money, they become, what one writer calls, "leakages of power." We assume that Christ's followers will condemn gross evil, but "the heart of holy living," wrote William Law (*Serious Call to a Devout and Holy Life*), "chiefly consists in the right and prudent management of ourselves with respect to such matters which are neither commanded nor forbidden in the Word of God."

(b) Also, Christian liberty must be restricted when a practice, which may be quite lawful, threatens to take us captive. "All things are lawful for me, but I will not be enslaved by anything." How enslaved some believers are to sports, to TV, to politics, to making money, to good eating and dressing, or what have you! All these things have their appropriate place, but they can easily get us into bondage.

With these general comments on the limitations of Christian liberty Paul tackles the problem of fornication.

## II. Violations of Christian Liberty (6:13-17)

In Gnosticism the human body was denigrated. To combat this tendency in the Corinthian church Paul argues for the dignity of the human body.

(a) *The body belongs to the Lord* (v. 13). "Foods for the stomach and the stomach for foods," sounds like another Corinthian slogan. Evidently they argued that the body and everything pertaining to it belonged to the category of religiously indifferent things. No doubt Paul would have to agree that food is for the stomach and the stomach for food. However, he would firmly reject the corollary that "sexual relations are for the body and the body for sexual relations."

There's a lot of confused thinking in our day on the urges, drives, needs and desires of the body. Obviously we need to eat and drink and sleep if we are to survive. We must remember, however, that between man as he came from the hand of God and man as he is today, stands the story of his fall into sin. Therefore, to do what is "natural" to us, does not necessarily make it right, for we are sinners. And so there are limits to the indiscriminate expressions of sexual desire.

The body, Paul explains, is "for the Lord and the Lord is for the body" (v. 13). If our bodies belong to Christ we must treat them with honor. The Lord is for the body in the sense that he made it, he sustains it, and he will raise it some day. Obviously then the body is not for fornication.

Both foods and the stomach will be done away with when this age comes to an end, but the body will be raised up and transformed into a spiritual body.

(b) *The body will be raised up by God* (v. 14). Our bodies of flesh and blood are designed for this present age. But, they wear out; they are subject to disease and death. That, however, is not the end of the story. On the resurrection morning they will be raised up and transformed into the image of our glorious Lord. That same power which was manifested when God raised Christ from the dead will be demonstrated when the last trumpet sounds and the dead shall be raised incorruptible.

The resurrection body will be very different from our present "body of humiliation," as Paul calls it (Phil. 3:21), but there is a continuity between what we are now and what we shall be then. For that reason this mortal body must be treated with respect.

(c) *Our body is a member of Christ's body* (vv. 15-17). "Do you not know that your bodies are members of Christ? Shall I therefore take the members of Christ and make them members of a prostitute? Never"! (v. 15). Paul assumes that his readers know that believers are the limbs and organs of Christ's body. It is, therefore, terribly reprehensible to unite with a prostitute. Illicit sexual behavior desecrates the body and robs Christ of what is rightfully his. Lawful sexual union, within marriage, involves no such desecration; rather, it is an analogy of the church's union with Christ (Eph. 5:22ff.).

When a believer unites with a prostitute (Paul uses the verb "to glue") he becomes one body with her (v. 16). That this is so can be supported from the story of the creation of man and woman, where it is said: "The two shall become one flesh" (Gen. 2:24). A sexual relationship is not casual contact; it involves people's personalities in the profoundest sense.

To distinguish between a sexual union with another person and the union of the believer with his Lord, Paul adds: "But he who is united to the Lord is one *spirit* with him" (v. 17).

Sexual immorality, Paul argues, is an outrage because the believer's body belongs to Christ, his body has a glorious destiny, and his body (meaning the person) is a member of the body of Christ.

After showing his readers the limitations of Christian liberty, and warning them against the violations of true Christian freedom, Paul exhorts them to practice true Christian liberty, which is very different from license.

### III. Practice of True Christian Liberty (6:18-20)

The apostle gives three reasons why the Corinthians should refrain from illicit sexual relations and to discover true freedom in Christ.

(a) *Because of the gravity of the sin* (v. 18). Other sins, Paul explains, are done outside the body, but the one who fornicates, sins against his own body. For that reason believers should "flee from fornication" — an echo, perhaps, of Joseph's literal fleeing from temptation (Gen. 39:12). This has sometimes been called "the flight of a hero," and not the flight of a coward. It calls for courage and strength to live chastely in an immoral society.

But how can Paul say that sins, other than fornication, are done outside the body? Does not drunkenness or gluttony involve the body in a similar way? One answer is that eating and drinking are perfectly good activities and become sinful only when done in excess, whereas fornication is always sinful. Another view is that

drunkenness and gluttony affect only the individual, whereas fornication has permanent effects on at least two people (usually more
than two are hurt). Perhaps Paul is simply using Jewish ter-
minology, for sexual sin was called "sinning with the body."

In any case, fornication is such a serious violation of per-
sonhood (for it is designed to satisfy lust), that Paul views it as particularly reprehensible. However, that should not be understood to
mean that sexual sins are unforgiveable, or that some other sins
cannot have an equally devastating effect on people.

(b) *Because of the sanctity of the body* (v. 19). True liberty in
Christ does not permit licentious living, for the believer's body is
a temple of the Holy Spirit. Again Paul assumes that his readers
know this. The word for temple is *naos,* meaning a sacred shrine
in which the deity dwells. God lives in the individual Christian by
his Spirit and so our bodies are the Spirit's temple.

The doctrine of creation gave a strong impulse to Jews and
Christians to have a high view of the body. Here, however, an even
stronger motive is suggested. If the Holy Spirit resides in us, then
it is monstrous if we abuse our bodies. In I Thessalonians 4:1ff.,
where Paul also warns against fornication, he strengthens his case
by saying that God *keeps* on giving (us) his Holy Spirit" (v. 8).

In the letters of Ignatius (ca. 112 A.D.), the bishop speaks of
himself as *christophoros* (a bearer of Christ — our "Christopher"),
*theophoros* (a bearer of God),and *naophoros* (a bearer of a sacred
shrine). In his letter to the Ephesians he writes: "Let us do all things
in the conviction he dwells in us. Thus we shall be his temple and
he will be our God within us."

Since God has taken up residence in our bodies by his Spirit,
we do not belong to ourselves. Whether we live or die we are the
Lord's, and so we can't do with our bodies as we please. We are
but stewards of that which belongs to God.

(c) *Because of the costliness of redemption* (v. 20). A final reason
why the body of the Christian should not be degraded by sexual immorality is that the body has been redeemed by Christ at a great
cost. Gnostics might argue that only the spirit was saved; Paul insists that Christ's redemption embraces our bodies, too. "You were
bought with a price. So glorify God in your body."

The language Paul uses in our passage is taken, so it seems,
from the practice of sacred manumission, by which slaves could

earn their freedom by depositing their purchase price at a sacred shrine, being freed, as it were, by the deity. Paul's language in verse 20 has been found in inscriptions.

The price of our purchase is Christ's blood (as Revelation 5:9 has it: "by thy blood (thou) didst ransom men for God"). And because the cost of our redemption is so high, and since redemption embraces also the body (the final stage of that redemption is, of course, still future, Romans 8:23), we must glorify God in our bodies. They are, in fact, the only instruments we have by which we can glorify God here on earth.

The King James Version has an interesting addition in verse 20: "Glorify God in your body *and in your spirit, which are God's.*" This addition has poor manuscript support, and is obviously an addition by a copyist who wanted to soften Paul's abrupt close and to extend the range of Paul's application.

The entire paragraph focuses on the body of the believer, which has been created and redeemed, and which shall be changed some day to a glorious body. Until that day comes we can live in the liberty with which Christ has set us free and not in the bondage which comes from licentious living.

## Personal Response

1. *Paul says we should not allow any practice to control us (v. 12). What are some things, practices, or relationships that may enslave us? How do we know when a certain thing, practice, or relationship has enslaved us? What are the steps to enslavement? What are steps out of enslavement?*
2. *Sexual immorality comes under special consideration here. Why?*
3. *Other than physical intimacy, what are some sexually immoral behaviors that people, including believers, may engage in? How can we avoid these?*
4. *How can we teach and encourage our youth to live pure lives in a world filled with sexually immoral influences?*

# CHAPTER TEN

## The Sanctity of Marriage

*Now for the matters you wrote about: It is good for a man not to marry. But since there is so much immorality, each man should have his own wife, and each woman her own husband. The husband should fulfill his marital duty to his wife, and likewise the wife to her husband. The wife's body does not belong to her alone but also to her husband. In the same way, the husband's body does not belong to him alone but also to his wife. Do not deprive each other except by mutual consent and for a time, so that you may devote yourselves to prayer. Then come together again so that Satan will not tempt you because of your lack of self-control. I say this as a concession, not as a command. I wish that all men were as I am. But each man has his own gift from God; one has this gift, another has that.*

*Now to the unmarried and the widows I say: It is good for them to stay unmarried, as I am. But if they cannot control themselves, they should marry, for it is better to marry than to burn with passion.*

*To the married I give this command (not I, but the Lord): A wife must not separate from her husband. But if she does, she must remain unmarried or else be reconciled to her husband. And a husband must not divorce his wife.*

*To the rest I say this (I, not the Lord): If any brother has a wife who is not a believer and she is willing to live with him, he must*

*not divorce her. And if a woman has a husband who is not a believer
and he is willing to live with her, she must not divorce him. For the
unbelieving husband has been sanctified through his wife, and the
unbelieving wife has been sanctified through her believing husband.
Otherwise your children would be unclean, but as it is, they are holy.*

*But if the unbeliever leaves, let him do so. A believing man or
woman is not bound in such circumstances; God has called us to
live in peace. How do you know, wife, whether you will save your
husband? Or, how do you know, husband, whether you will save
your wife? (I Corinthians 7:1-16).*

While ministering at Ephesus, the apostle Paul received a letter
from the Corinthian congregation. In this letter he was asked questions about marriage and divorce (7:1), virginity (7:25), food offered
to idols (8:1), spiritual gifts (12:1), the collection for Jerusalem (16:1)
and Apollos (16:12). The first part of chapter seven answers the first
question.

After dealing with licentious tendencies in chapters five and
six, Paul now seems to combat a false asceticism. He fights on two
fronts. In Gnosticism both of these opposing emphases were found.
If the body is evil and only the spirit is good, then it does not matter
how much one indulges the body. On the other hand, if the body
is evil, then its desires have to be put under strict control, leading
to asceticism.

In chapter seven Paul deals with the ascetics who, perhaps in
reaction to the libertines, argued that all sexual relations were to be
deprecated. His concern is that the sanctity of the marriage relationship be preserved.

### I. Marriage and Celibacy (7:1-7)

"It is well for a man not to touch a woman" (v. 1) is probably
a quotation from the Corinthians' letter, and represents the ascetic
viewpoint. To "touch" is a euphemism for sexual relations (sexual
relations outside of marriage have been condemned in chapter 6).

Paul agrees that the celibate state is good. There is nothing
blameworthy about being single. The rabbis generally felt differently about that, and some wondered whether an unmarried
man could attain to eternal life. But Paul has left his rabbinic views
on this behind. Celibate people, too, can live a rich and meaningful
life in the Lord.

However, while singleness is not in any way condemned, Paul advises his readers to marry (v. 2). Marriage is a protection against unchastity, he argues. Fornication abounded in Corinth and so he advises people to marry. That Paul holds to monogamous marriage is clear from verse 2.

The apostle has been faulted for a low view of marriage, but such a charge is without foundation. There is no New Testament writer who has such a high view of marriage as the one who wrote Ephesians 5:21-33. In I Corinthians 7 he is answering questions, and one cannot say everything about a topic in reply to a question.

It appears from what Paul says in verses 3 and 4, that marriage partners in Corinth wondered whether sexual relations in marriage were legitimate or not. Paul instructs husband and wife to fulfill their conjugal obligations one to another (v. 3). Do notice that Paul does not speak of the husband's or the wife's "rights," but of their duties. By the marriage vow both husband and wife relinquish exclusive rights to their own bodies. "For the wife does not rule over her own body, but the husband does; likewise, the husband does not rule over his own body, but the wife does" (v. 4). In the matter of conjugal relations there is complete equality.

Having endorsed the marriage relationship, Paul now cautions husbands and wives not to defraud one another (v. 5). There may, of course, be times when husband and wife by mutual agreement abstain from sexual relations, in order to give themselves to prayer. The apostle cautions, however, that well-intentioned expressions of piety, if carried too far, can be exploited by the adversary to bring about moral disaster.

This, however, Paul says by way of concession (v. 6). Precisely what he has in mind is not clear, but probably the suggestion to separate temporarily for the purpose of prayer is meant.

But, in spite of his high view of marriage Paul insists that the celibate state cannot be faulted. Indeed, he expresses the wish that all men might be as he is (v. 7). The Paul who meets us on the pages of the New Testament is not married. Whether he had been married at one time is not known. The silly notion that he married Lydia of Philippi, and that she is addressed as his "true yoke fellow" (Phil. 4:3), puts too great a strain on our imagination.

Does Paul then wish that all believers be single? C.K. Barrett suggests that Paul meant the gift of living chastely in a society full of sexual allurements. Perhaps Paul had Jesus' words about those who were "eunuchs for the sake of the kingdom" (Mt. 19:12) in mind. To live the celibate life calls for a *charisma* (v. 7), just as marriage and parenthood call for it. Both marriage and singleness, then, are legitimate states, with marriage being the normal state.

## II. Unmarried and Married (7:8-11)

Paul now addresses different groups in the church. First, the unmarried (men) and widows are told that there is nothing reprehensible about their state (v. 8). Precisely why Paul thought it was better for them to remain as he was is not stated. Was it because the times were so turbulent (v. 26), or was it in order to devote themselves wholly to the Lord's work? In any case, he recognizes that not all have his *charisma*, and so it's better if bachelors, widowers and widows marry (unmarried girls will be treated later in the chapter).

Living in a licentious society, where sexual passions are constantly aroused, it is better to marry than to burn (v. 9). Usually that is taken to mean to "burn with passion," but it could possibly also mean to "burn in hell" because of fornication (Mt. 5:28,29).

But what about Christians who are married? (vv. 10,11). Paul had to deal with numerous problems that emerged in the life of the church in the Gentile world which Jesus had never addressed directly. However, Jesus had spoken of the permanence of the marriage covenant, and so Paul can quote Jesus in his answer to this question. Jesus had taught that there was to be no divorce (Mt. 5:32; 19:9; Mk. 10:9, Lk. 16:18), and Paul can speak not only on his own authority on this matter, but by the authority of Jesus.

"The wife should not separate from her husband (but if she does, let her remain single or else be reconciled to her husband) — and that the husband should not divorce his wife" (vv. 10,11). Like Jesus, Paul holds to the creation ideal that husband and wife should not separate (the distinction between separation and divorce in our modern legal system is irrelevant in understanding the biblical texts dealing with divorce and remarriage).

Having stated the creation ideal, that there should be no divorce, Paul recognizes that human sinfulness often leads to the breakup of a marriage relationship. That Paul should warn first the wife and then the husband against divorce can be explained perhaps by the sequence of the Corinthian questions. In Israel the wife did not have the freedom to initiate divorce as did women in the Greco-Roman world.

What shall a Christian spouse do when the marriage covenant has been violated and a separation has taken place? Paul's counsel to the wife who left her husband is that she should not marry another man (that would be adultery, Mk. 10:12), but that she be reconciled to him. It is assumed, of course, that her husband has not yet married. What she shall do if reconciliation fails and her husband marries another woman is not stated in our text. (Presumably what is said to the woman would apply equally to the man.)

With the massive break-down in marriages in our day the church should do all it can to stress the permanence of the marriage covenant and to strengthen those marriages which seem to be faltering. Also, it must learn to treat with compassion those whose marriages have collapsed. One can hold unwaveringly to the biblical teachings on marriage and at the same time, proclaim the gospel of God's forgiveness to those who have failed in their marriage.

### III. Mixed Marriages (7:12-16)

There were also those in the Corinthian church who had married before their conversion, and Paul now speaks to them. In one case the wife accepted the gospel and her husband did not; in the other, the husband accepted the gospel and the wife remained an unbeliever. The Corinthians must have asked whether such a marriage (of believer and unbeliever) was still a legitimate marriage, or whether the Christian partner should leave her unbelieving spouse.

Since Paul cannot quote a saying of Jesus on this matter (for Jesus had not addressed this issue) he must give his own instructions. "I say, not the Lord" (v. 12). This does not make Paul's teachings less authoritative, for he speaks as Christ's apostle who has the Spirit of God (v. 40).

Paul's instructions on "mixed" marriages do not deal with the question of whether it's right or advisable for a believer to choose an unbeliever for a marriage partner. Rather, he's addressing couples who were married before either of them heard the gospel, and where one of the partners had become a Christian. That such a relationship often put a great strain on the believing spouse can be seen from the writings of the early church fathers. Justin Martyr, for example, in his second Apology tells of a pagan husband who denounced his wife to the authorities when she as a Christian had left him because of his drunkenness and immorality.

What is Paul's message to believers who have unbelieving spouses? The believer is not to leave the unbelieving partner if this partner is content to continue the marriage relationship (vv. 12,13). Since marriage is for all mankind, believers and unbelievers alike, there is nothing illegitimate about the marriage of a believer to an unbeliever. Marriage is a creation order not, in the first instance, a Christian institution. And so Paul does not encourage Christian spouses to leave their unbelieving partners. Christian legend has it that the apostle Andrew was crucified because he had encouraged Christian wives to leave their pagan husbands.

To encourage believing spouses to stay with their unbelieving partners Paul explains that "the unbelieving husband is consecrated through his wife, and the unbelieving wife is consecrated through her husband. Otherwise your children would be unclean, but as it is they are holy" (v. 14). The believer is not defiled by his or her association with an unbelieving partner. Rather, the unbelieving partner comes under the hallowing influence of the believer. Not only is a mixed marriage legitimate, but the believing spouse exercises a sacred influence. If a mixed marriage were not legitimate then the children of such a marriage would not be legitimate. Now, however, they are "holy." This does not mean that children who have Christian parents, or one Christian parent, are automatically saved. That the passage has nothing to do with paedo-baptism is also clear. Paul doesn't say that baptized babies are holy. But on the Old Testament principle that "whatever touches the altar shall be holy" (Ex. 29:37), a child of a Christian parent is under a sacred influence.

Therefore, since a mixed marriage is quite proper, as far as the marriage is concerned, and children of such partners are legitimate children under the sign of God's grace because of a believing parent, the believing spouse should not leave the unbelieving partner.

If, however, the unbelieving partner insists on separating from his believing spouse, then "the brother or sister is not bound" (v., 15).

This seems to imply that the believer would be free to marry again, although Paul does not say so explicitly. F.F. Bruce (Commentary, p. 70) is of the opinion that such a rejected Christian wife is in the state of widowhood and might remarry. In any case, she is not bound to remain with her unbelieving husband if he does not want her.

Since God has called us to peace (v. 15), the believer should stay with the unbelieving partner as long as he or she allows it. If not, then the believing spouse must accept the tragedy of being divorced.

To those who might be too quick to leave the unbelieving partner Paul points out the possibility of winning the unbeliever over to the faith (v. 16). Others, however, read verse 16 to mean that the believing spouse should not insist on remaining with an unbelieving partner in the hope of winning the unbeliever, for that prospect is rather dim (so the RSV).

Christians should not enter a marriage with an unbeliever in the hope of winning him or her to Christ. Where, however, a mixed marriage exists, the believer must seek to live in such a way that the unbeliever is attracted to the Christian faith. To discover how this is to be done one needs to read I Peter 3:1-6.

### *Personal Response*

1. *The church seemingly stands alone in the belief in the permanence of marriage (vv. 10-11). What can churches do to stress the permanence of marriage and to strengthen those marriages which may be in difficulty?*
2. *Marriages involving believers and unbelievers are most difficult situations (vv. 12-16). What attitudes and characteristics must a believing partner have in a mixed marriage? How can the church stand along side a believing partner? What should be the attitude of the church toward the unbelieving partner?*
3. *What should be the attitude of the church toward those whose marriages have failed? How can the church help these people?*
4. *List attitudes and influences which lead to the breakup of marriages. Which do you think is most important?*

# CHAPTER ELEVEN

## On Personal and Family Matters

*Nevertheless, each one should retain the place in life that the Lord assigned to him and to which God has called him. This is the rule I lay down in all the churches. Was a man already circumcised when he was called? He should not become uncircumcised. Was a man uncircumcised when he was called? He should not be circumcised. Circumcision is nothing and uncircumcision is nothing. Keeping God's commands is what counts. Each one should remain in the situation which he was in when God called him. Were you a slave when you were called? Don't let it trouble you — although if you can gain your freedom, do so. For he who was a slave when he was called by the Lord is the Lord's freedman; similarly, he who was a free man when he was called is Christ's slave. You were bought at a price; do not become slaves of men. Brothers, each man, as responsible to God, should remain in the situation God called him to.*

*Now about virgins: I have no command from the Lord, but I give a judgment as one who by the Lord's mercy is trustworthy. Because of the present crisis, I think that it is good for you to remain as you are. Are you married? Do not seek a divorce. Are you unmarried? Do not look for a wife. But if you do marry, you have not sinned; and if a virgin marries, she has not sinned. But those who marry will face many troubles in this life, and I want to spare you this.*

*What I mean, brothers is that the time is short. From now on*

*those who have wives should live as if they had none; those who
mourn, as if they did not; those who are happy, as if they were not;
those who buy something, as if it were not theirs to keep; those who
use the things of the world, as if not engrossed in them. For this
world in its present form is passing away.*

*I would like you to be free from concern. An unmarried man
is concerned about the Lord's affairs — how he can please the Lord.
But a married man is concerned about the affairs of this world —
how he can please his wife — and his interests are divided. An unmarried woman or virgin is concerned about the Lord's affairs: Her
aim is to be devoted to the Lord in both body and spirit. But a married woman is concerned about the affairs of this world — how she
can please her husband. I am saying this for your own good, not to
restrict you, but that you may live in a right way in undivided devotion to the Lord.*

*If anyone thinks he is acting improperly toward the virgin he is
engaged to, and if she is getting along in years and he feels he ought
to marry, he should do as he wants. He is not sinning. They should
get married. But the man who has settled the matter in his own
mind, who is under no compulsion but has control over his own will,
and who has made up his mind not to marry the virgin — this man
also does the right thing. So then, he who marries the virgin does
right, but he who does not marry her does even better.*

*A woman is bound to her husband as long as he lives. But if
her husband dies, she is free to marry anyone she wishes, but he
must belong to the Lord. In my judgment, she is happier if she stays
as she is — and I think that I too have the Spirit of God (I Corinthians 7:17-40).*

The entire seventh chapter of I Corinthians is devoted to questions concerning marriage and celibacy. The verses 17-24,
however, do not appear to fit this theme and may have to be viewed as a digression. This paragraph answers the question: How does
the call of the gospel affect a believer's social status?

One could argue, of course, that this question is part and parcel
of the larger discussion. Just as a believing marriage partner is not
released from her or his spouse by conversion to Christ (vv. 12-16),
so a slave is not automatically released from his master when he
responds to the gospel. Or, perhaps in contrast to mixed marriages,
where the unbelieving partner may take the initiative and end his
or her marriage to the believing spouse, no such radical changes are

demanded in other areas of one's life.

Be that as it may, Paul has some wise counsel to give to those who had asked questions on how faith in Christ affects one's station in life.

### I. Counsel on One's Calling (7:17-24)

In Paul's day, as in ours, the gospel came to people in all kinds of life-situations. One might be a carpenter, another a housewife, still another a theater attendant, or what have you. The question for these new converts was: Must we leave our jobs, our professions, our stations in life? Paul's answer in general is: "Let every one lead the life which the Lord has assigned to him, and in which God has called him" (7:17). This, adds Paul, is his practice in all the churches.

If we are allowed to include the previous paragraph, Paul's counsel is: If a person is married, conversion does not ask him to break the marriage relationship. In the light of the following verses, Paul's rule of thumb is that the conversion of a Gentile does not ask for his circumcision, any more than the conversion of a Jew calls for "uncircumcision." (There are references to an operation by which renegade Jewish males tried to undo their circumcision. See I Macc. 1:15; Josephus, *Ant.* XII.V.1).

Moreover, when a slave heard the gospel and believed, he was not now to make a break for freedom, although Paul seems to encourage slaves to grasp the opportunity if they can (v. 21). And vice versa a free person should not feel obligated to become a slave because of his conversion to Christ.

The general rule is that people should remain in the socioeconomic situation in which they were when Christ found them. This rule must, however, not be made absolute. Paul is not suggesting that it is wrong to leave one profession for another after conversion. Nor is he counselling against efforts to improve one's economic situation. Moreover, the church very early recognized that there were disreputable professions which Christians must forsake upon conversion. The third century *Apostolic Constitutions* of Hippolytus have a long list of professions which Christians were to avoid.

Nevertheless, Paul's rule, that conversion does not demand a change in one's social or economic status, holds even for us.

In Paul's day it must have been an acute question for a Gentile male convert whether he should not take on circumcision. After all, "Salvation [was] from the Jews," and Gentiles who joined the Jewish synagogues as proselytes took on circumcision.

On the other hand, Jews, who were circuncised and who accepted Jesus as the Messiah, recognized that they had broken with traditional Judaism. They may have wondered whether or not they should put their past completely behind them by erasing even the marks of circumcision (v. 18).

Paul's answer is no! Circumcision or foreskin play no role in the church (v. 19). Paul is not slighting the sacred sign of the old covenant, but with the establishment of the new covenant in Christ the mark of a true covenant member is not circumcision but obedience to God's commands (v. 19). Old Testament prophets had in fact anticipated this Pauline position by insisting that without obedience to the covenant the outward sign of the covenant was meaningless. Whatever a person's social status may be, when he hears God's call in the gospel, he must remain true to this call, circumcised or not (v. 20).

Similarly, when a slave heard the call of the gospel and accepted Christ he was not to chafe under this condition and think that the blessings of salvation were being withheld from him because he was a slave. Should release become possible a slave might well seek freedom (v. 21).

Slavery and freedom must be viewed from the perspective of the Lordship of Christ. At conversion the slave receives a new master, Jesus Christ, who sets him free from the bondage of sin and death, and so the Christian slave is a free person even though he has an earthly master and serves his earthly master as a free person (Eph. 6:5ff). Vice versa, a free person, who accepts Christ, can no longer live in independence, for he has voluntarily submitted himself to a new master, Christ (v. 22).

Jesus paid a high price to make mankind free (see I Cor. 6:20), and so Paul's counsel is, to both slaves and free, not to live in bondage to man, neither literally nor spiritually. Purchased at infinite cost believers owe supreme loyalty to Christ and must not allow themselves to be enslaved by the social, materialistic and hedonistic values of a pagan society (v. 23).

Repeating the injunctions of verses 17 and 20, Paul underscores once more that each convert is to remain in the state in which God calls him by the gospel — with this added note: "with God." Marriage to an unbelieving spouse, working as a slave for an earthly master, uncongenial or congenial life-situations, are transformed when lived in "the presence of God" (v. 24).

## II. Counsel for the Unmarried (7:25-38)

The opening words of this paragraph ("now concerning") suggest that the Corinthians had asked a question about "virgins." Whereas the word "virgin" (*parthenos*) can apply to both male and female in both a literal and metaphorical sense (see Rev. 14:4). In our passage it seems to be restricted to unmarried women. If verse 34 distinguishes between the *parthenos* and the unmarried woman, we may have to think of a particular category of unmarried girls, perhaps the betrothed but not yet married. The question of the Corinthians seems to have been: Should betrothed girls proceed to marriage or should they refrain?

Paul admits that he has no command from the Lord on this question. Our Lord had no occasion to speak to this issue, and Paul did not feel free to invent sayings of Jesus. This did not mean, of course, that what Paul taught was less authoritative but, since marriage is a creation order, Paul can only give advice on whether betrothed girls should marry or not. His advice even in such matters, however, is not to be treated lightly since God in his mercy made him an apostle (v. 25).

(a) *His Counsel* (26-28). Paul suggests that in view of the current distress it were better if marriage were delayed. Unfortunately it is not clear to us what "distress" Paul had in mind. Since persecution was the lot of Christians from the beginning Paul may have had a time of great trial in mind in which marriage would only add to the burdens of persecuted believers.

If, as some hold, Paul expected the great tribulation prior to Christ's coming (see II Thess. 2:1ff) to come upon the church at any moment, and for this reason advised against marriage, his counsel becomes very problematic for the church always lives in the last hour and Christians are nowhere else advised to refrain from marriage because the coming of the Lord is near.

It may be best to think simply of some unusually difficult circumstances in which Paul's readers found themselves and that

Paul, out of pastoral concerns, advises married and unmarried people alike to remain as they are. Decisions that affect one's entire life are best not made in the midst of turmoil (vv. 26-27).

Paul recognizes, of course, that it is not wrong to marry even when the times are out of joint (v. 28) but those who do may have added "affliction in the flesh." Troublesome times tend to put extra burdens on married couples and their children. In the words of Francis Bacon: "Children sweeten labors, but make misfortunes more bitter."

(b) *Perspectives for His Counsel* (29-31). Paul sees everything from the standpoint of eternity and so he not only gives his advice to unmarried girls from that perspective but calls on his readers also to look at things in the light of the dawn of the age to come. Since time is short and the end is always near, the believer must temper his life on earth by eternal values. The joys and sorrows of life, the procuring and the use of earthly goods, must all be seen in the light of the brevity and the ephemeral nature of this age which is passing away.

(c) *Purpose of His Counsel* (32-35). With that perspective, Paul returns to the subject under discussion. Since the burdens of family life are intensified in times of trouble, Paul advises his readers not to change their married (or unmarried) state. The reason is he wants them to be without anxieties.

Unmarried men are less divided in their interests and can devote themselves completely to the Lord's service (v. 32). The married man, by contrast, has to concern himself with worldly affairs as well; he has to take care of his family. Not that this is wrong, for if one is not willing to pay attention to the needs of wife and children one's understanding of marriage is warped.

Similarly, the married woman is anxious about worldly affairs. She has to care for her husband and her children; she must feed and clothe them, and so she too is divided in her interests. The single girl can devote herself completely, body and spirit, to the Lord.

Again Paul is not saying that the unmarried state makes for a higher degree of holiness, but he is realistic enough to recognize that married people have to spend time and energy in earthly cares in a way the unmarried do not, and consequently cannot spend all their energy in so-called Christian service.

Paul's advice to the unmarried girls is, therefore, to remain

single in this time of distress and to devote themselves to Christ and
his kingdom. However, they are not obligated to follow Paul's advice. Paul is only concerned about their welfare. In no way does he
want to put a noose around their necks. On the contrary, he wants
to promote good order and relieve his hearers of burdensome
distractions (v. 35). For this reason, also, he adds some qualifications to his instructions.

(d) *Some Qualifications* (36-38). The following paragraph bristles
with difficulties and perhaps the best we can do is to give several
lines of interpretation and then choose the one which seems most
likely to be correct. If, in spite of Paul's counsel, someone is per-
suaded that it's better that his girl ("virgin") should marry, he does
not sin. On the other hand, if someone makes the opposite decision,
he does not sin either, although, given the current circumstances,
Paul thinks his decision is the wiser one. The question, therefore,
is of a practical rather than of a moral nature.

But who is the "someone" who is to make this decision? Is it
the father of the girl? Fathers did have a whole lot to say in those
days about the marriage of their daughters. Or, is it her fiancé? A
third view is that Paul has the practice of "spiritual" marriage in
mind and that by getting married Paul means here that the husband
decides to enter into a physical relationship with his wife, after
agreeing with her to live as brother and sister in Christ. Spiritual
marriages are, however, not attested as early as the middle of the
first century; they were a later phenomenon.

The answer to our question depends somewhat on our
understanding of the adjective *hyperakmos* (v. 36), (past one's
prime?). A father may decide to get a husband for his daughter
because she is getting "beyond marriageable age" (as determined
by the culture of that day). Others say *hyperakmos* refers to sexual
passion, and the father wants his daughter to get married lest she
get into trouble. This meaning of *hyperakmos* would then also apply
to the marriage partners who had agreed to live in virginity one
with another, but found that strain too much, and the husband then
makes the decision to enter into what one might call a normal
marriage.

Perhaps if it were clear who is meant by the "virgin," the
answer would be easier. Is she the daughter (the *Jerusalem Bible*);
is she the fiancee (Today's English Version); or, is she a married

woman living in virginity with her husband?

In our view, the interpretation that is the least problematic is the one which takes the man who decides that the girl should either marry or not marry to be her father. The father who arranges for the marriage of his daughter even in turbulent times, because he's afraid that she will lose the bloom of youth, does not sin, says Paul. However, where there is no such pressure, he does better if he delays marriage, is Paul's advice.

### III. Counsel for Widows (7:39-40)

Paul holds that marriage is for life. Therefore, a wife is bound to her husband, for better or for worse, until death does them part. If the husband dies, however, she is free to marry whom she wishes, as long as she marries "in the Lord" (v. 39). Whereas the text does not say it explicitly, the implication seems to be that, if she exercises her freedom to remarry, she should marry a Christian man. In Paul's opinion (perhaps also in the light of the current distress and the freedom to devote herself completely to God's cause) she would do better if she did not marry.

And lest anyone take Paul's advice too lightly, he reminds his readers that he also has the Spirit of God. There seem to have been some hyper-spiritual men in Corinth who laid down the law in the matters Paul has just discussed, and that may be the reason the Corinthians had submitted these questions to Paul. The apostle will not command where he has not been given authority by his Lord to do so, but God's Spirit has enabled him to counsel his readers in such delicate matters with spiritual wisdom.

Whereas some of the questions which Paul addresses in this chapter may have arisen out of a pioneer situation, much of what Paul has to say is still very relevant to our situation today and is worth pondering and observing.

### *Personal Response*

1. *Paul writes about "retain(ing) the place in life" that a person was in when he/she became a believer (v. 17). What things change and what things do not change when a person becomes a believer?*
2. *What, if any, professions are unsuitable for believers? Why?*
3. *Paul seems to encourage a single life (vv. 25-35). Singleness is becom-*

ing more common today than in the past. How can the church accept
single people into full participation in the church?
4. What considerations does Paul raise for or against marriage? How
can a person balance concern for the family, the kingdom of God,
and the need to earn a livelihood in today's fast-paced world?

# CHAPTER TWELVE

## Love and Knowledge

*Now about food sacrificed to idols: We know that we all possess knowledge. Knowledge puffs up, but love builds up. The man who thinks he knows something does not yet know as he ought to know. But the man who loves God is known by God.*

*So then, about eating food sacrificed to idols: We know that an idol is nothing at all in the world and that there is no God but one. For even if there are so-called gods, whether in heaven or on earth (as indeed there are many "gods" and many "lords"), yet for us there is but one God, the Father, from whom all things came and for whom we live; and there is but one Lord, Jesus Christ, through whom all things came and through whom we live. But not everyone knows this. Some people are still so accustomed to idols that when they eat such food they think of it as having been sacrificed to an idol, and since their conscience is weak, it is defiled. But food does not bring us near to God; we are no worse if we do not eat, and no better if we do.*

*Be careful, however, that the exercise of your freedom does not become a stumbling block to the weak. For if anyone with a weak conscience sees you who have this knowledge eating in an idol's temple, won't he be emboldened to eat what has been sacrificed to idols? So this weak brother, for whom Christ died, is destroyed by your knowledge. When you sin against your brothers in this way and wound their weak conscience, you sin against Christ.*

> *Therefore, if what I eat causes my brother to fall into sin, I will*
> *never eat meat again, so that I will not cause him to fall (I Corin-*
> *thians 8:1-13).*

The opening words of chapter 8 suggest that Paul is answering another question which the Corinthians had asked him (compare 8:1 with 7:1, "now concerning the things about which you wrote"). That the question was significant can be gathered from Paul's rather long answer. Chapters 8,9 and 10 are devoted to the question of meat sacrificed to idols.

A modern reader might be inclined to dismiss these chapters as irrelevant. However, on further reflection, one discovers much in Paul's answer that is of permanent validity for the Christian life. These chapters raise the question of Christian liberty, of living without offence in the Christian community; they show us how conscience functions; in fact they deal with that ever-current issue of how a believer is to live in a sinful society.

Chapter 8 introduces the topic, chapter 9 offers a personal illustration, and chapter 10 gives some practical guidelines on how to live a godly life in a pagan world (and Corinth and North America are not too different in that regard).

It was a practice in pagan temples to sacrifice animals to the gods. The deity received a portion, the priests and temple attendants got a share, and what was left over was sold to the public. The question now was: Could Christians buy this meat at the market? Besides, even domestic butchering of animals was tainted by idolatrous practices. Moreover, it was common to have meals with friends in the temple precincts and so the believer would have to ask whether it was fitting for him to dine with friends in an idol temple. Or, if an unbelieving friend invited him to dinner, should he go? What if he served meat dedicated to the gods? These and many other questions were related to the topic under discussion in these chapters.

Paul points out that such complex issues can be solved only where there is a loving relationship between believers. In fact he begins by showing the relationship between love and knowledge.

## I. The Limits of Knowledge (8:1-3)
"Now concerning food offered to idols we know that all of us

possess knowledge" (v. 1). Whether this opening sentence is a quotation from the Corinthian letter, representing the thinking of the progressive church member, or whether there's a touch of irony in this statement is not quite clear. In a moment Paul will tell us what kind of knowledge he's talking about. It is the knowledge that there is only one God and that idols don't represent real gods and that, therefore, the whole question of meat offered to idols is irrelevant. Those who had come to this insight may have scorned those who still had conscience scruples about such matters.

Paul sides with those who have come to the conviction that an idol is nothing but the danger is that these liberated people will become puffed up (a besetting sin of the Corinthians; see 4:6,18,19; 5:2). The concern of the believer, however, should be to build one another up and that happens only where people love each other.

Moreover, Paul reminds his readers that "if anyone imagines that he knows something, he does not yet know as he ought to know" (v. 2). This observation holds for knowledge in general as much as it does for the particular kind of knowledge Paul has in mind. People who are well-informed on a given subject are often quite humble for they know how much more there is to know about their area of expertise.

The progressive Corinthian had made an important discovery. He had looked through the sham of idolatry; his faith in one God had made the question of meat offered to idols irrelevant. Paul cautions that perhaps he hasn't thought deeply enough. There are ramifications of this subject he may have overlooked. The problem was more complex than he realized. He'd better think a little harder.

Besides, the Corinthian who has come to this new understanding should remember that ethical questions cannot be settled cerebrally, by logic, by rational argument alone. The answers must flow out of a loving relationship with God. And such a relationship is possible only where God in his infinite love and mercy takes the initiative and chooses us ("knows" us) to be his children (v. 3). In debating ethical issues, then, we must be sure that we stand in a loving relationship with God and our brother.

## II. The Content of Knowledge (8:4-6)

"As to the eating of food offered to idols we know that an idol has no real existence and that there is no real God but one" (v. 4).

Paul identifies with the "strong" Corinthian who has come to this conviction that an idol is nothing. The word "idol" (*eidolon*) means "that which is seen," for the image of wood or stone is the visible representation of the invisible god.

One of the first things a Jewish boy learned for memory was the *Shema,* Israel's confession of faith, which begins: "Hear, O Israel, the Lord our God is one Lord." This strict monotheism was carried over into the Christian gospel and one can easily see how this could lead to an outright denial of the existence of other gods.

In pagan religion, however, these gods are taken seriously, "There are many so-called gods, in heaven or on earth" (v. 5). Greeks spoke of the Olympian (*uranian*) gods, who lived high on Mt. Olympus, and the *chthonian* (*chthon* means "earth") gods. They had a multitude of gods, whom they called "lords," ascribing deity to them. These gods were for the idol worshipers a living reality.

For the Christian believer, of course, argues Paul, "there is but one God, the Father" (v. 6). This was a new dimension in the gospel of Jesus Christ that the God who created the world and who had made Israel his people is our Father. Whereas Judaism put emphasis on the distance between God and man, and the Greek gods were by and large unfriendly deities who had to be humored by their devotees, the God our Lord Jesus Christ has become our Father.

This one God is not only the source of all things that exist but he is also the goal of our existence. Moreover, the unicity of God is not threatened by the confession that Jesus Christ is divine. It is in fact through him that not only the old creation but also the new creation, the church, has come into existence.

Whereas Paul shares the conviction with the "strong" Corinthian that there is but one God, he realizes that there are others in the church who have not yet seen the implications of such a faith. In fact this newly discovered knowledge has hidden dangers in it when it is not tempered by other considerations.

### III. The Dangers of Knowledge (8:7-13)

(a) *To cause one's brother to stumble* (8:7-9). Those Corinthians who had come out of paganism where idol worship was taken seriously could not overnight free themselves from the feeling that meat offered to idols was out of bounds for them. If such Corinthians eat meat dedicated to idols, "their conscience, being weak, is defiled" (v. 7). Through long custom the reality of the invisible god, represented by the visible idol, had been engrained on their consciences and they could not immediately shake this off. Jewish converts, of course, had a long tradition of a separation from all idolatry and would find it hard to act as if idols did not exist. (Jews had their own slaughter houses.)

The word "conscience" in Greek (as in Latin) means "to know together." (In the Old Testament the word is not found but the word "heart" in Hebrew embraces the functions of conscience.) This is instructive for our understanding of how conscience functions. Conscience always functions in keeping with "knowledge." Conscience condemns us if we violate what we have come to know as right and it commends us if we live in accord with this understanding. And while it is important that we have a good conscience, conscience is not a trustworthy guide. A conscience that is misinformed could for example lead Paul to persecute Christians when he was still an unbeliever and do so with a good conscience.

How then shall brothers and sisters in the same congregation live peaceably one with another when the conscience of some allows them to do things that others can't do? Paul makes some pertinent suggestions.

First, he seeks to enlighten his readers by reminding them that what we eat does not bring us closer to God. Vice versa, the eating of certain foods will not undermine our relationship with God. Foods are really a neutral matter. Paul follows Jesus at this point who by his discourse on foods "declared all foods to be clean" (Mark 7:9).

The Corinthian who has no pangs of conscience when he buys meat that was dedicated to idols is not more acceptable to God than the one who has scruples (and vice versa). However, the strong Corinthian, by his freedom, can encourage his brother who has scruples about eating idol meat, to eat also. This would harm the weaker brother. His freedom then becomes an occasion for his brother to stumble.

To be a stumbling block does not simply mean that someone in the congregation does not like what we do (how could we ever live in such a way that everyone would appreciate everything we did?). It means rather to encourage someone by word or example to do something that violates his conscience. That is harmful.

(b) *To cause the ruin of the brother* (8:10,11). Here's what might happen. A Christian with knowledge (i.e., that there is but one God and, therefore, the idol is nothing) gets an invitation to dine with a friend in a temple. (Archaeologists have discovered invitation cards that say just that.) He accepts the invitation and enjoys his meal without scruples.

This example encourages another person who does not yet have this freedom to do the same. For him this is not a neutral activity and his conscience bothers him. To violate conscience is so serious a matter for Paul that he condemns the liberated Corinthian for ruining and destroying his brother.

The strong Corinthian has acted according to his knowledge (a knowledge Paul shares) but he has not acted in love for his brother. This is all the more blameworthy when one remembers that it's a brother for whom Christ died (v. 11). To put it very pointedly: Christ laid down his life for the weak brother; you will not even lay down your fork and knife for him!

To encourage someone to violate his conscience is to cause him to stumble (8:7-9), to ruin him (vv. 10,11), and to sin against him (vv. 12,13). These are the dangers of knowledge where love is lacking.

(c) *To sin against the brother* (8:12,13). When someone sins against his brother by wounding his conscience, when it is weak, he really sins against Christ. Paul had learned that truth first when he was on the way to Damascus to persecute Christians. When the voice from heaven asked: "Saul, Saul, why do you persecute me?" it dawned on him that to hurt Christ's followers is to hurt Christ. So inextricably is Christ bound up with his own that to wound a Christian, weak though he may be, is to wound Christ.

Since this is so, Paul has decided that he will do everything within his power not to be a stumbling block to others. In fact, if food should be a cause of stumbling for his brother, he is willing to refrain from eating meat altogether.

The word for causing someone to stumble is *skandalizo* (our word scandal). Skandalon to begin with was the trap-stick on which the bait was put, by which one hoped to lure some creature into the trap. As Paul uses the word here it means to trip someone up in his Christian life by pushing him to act contrary to the voice of conscience.

Paul would rather be a vegetarian if by eating meat he encouraged his brother to violate his conscience.

In his understanding he is on the side of the strong but the law of love constrains him to live in such a manner that the weak are not hurt by his example. This attitude is a severe criticism of the individualism in ethical matters that so often characterizes the life of the church today. We do not live to ourselves and so we have to take into account the scruples, the feelings, the consciences of our brothers and sisters. May God help us to do this!

### Personal Response

1. *Paul speaks about food sacrificed to idols as a point of contention between believers. Name ethical situations where believers differ today.*
2. *What role should conscience play in making ethical decisions (v. 7)? What is the role of knowledge (v. 1)? How do conscience and knowledge work together?*
3. *Believers live in a church community and are concerned about each other (vv. 9-13). To what extent should the conscience of another believer determine our conduct? How should we relate to another believer when we have disagreements about ethical issues?*
4. *What is the responsibility of the church in deciding ethical issues?*

# CHAPTER THIRTEEN

## Paul Restricts His Rights

*Am I not free? Am I not an apostle? Have I not seen Jesus our Lord? Are you not the result of my work in the Lord? Even though I may not be an apostle to others, surely I am to you! For you are the seal of my apostleship in the Lord.*

*This is my defense to those who sit in judgment on me. Don't we have the right to food and drink? Don't we have the right to take a believing wife along with us, as do the other apostles and the Lord's brothers and Cephas? Or is it only I and Barnabas who must work for a living?*

*Who serves as a soldier at his own expense? Who plants a vineyard and does not eat of its grapes? Who tends a flock and does not drink of the milk? Do I say this merely from a human point of view? Doesn't the Law say the same thing? For it is written in the Law of Moses: "Do not muzzle an ox while it is treading out the grain." Is it about oxen that God is concerned? Surely he says this for us, doesn't he? Yes, this was written for us, because when the plowman plows and the thresher threshes, they ought to do so in the hope of sharing in the harvest. If we have sown spiritual seed among you, is it too much if we reap a material harvest from you? If others have this right of support from you, shouldn't we have it all the more?*

*But we did not use this right. On the contrary, we put up with anything rather than hinder the gospel of Christ. Don't you know that those who work in the temple get their food from the temple, and those who serve at the altar share in what is offered on the altar? In the same way, the Lord has commanded that those who preach the gospel should receive their living from the gospel.*

*But I have not used any of these rights. And I am not writing this in the hope that you will do such things for me. I would rather die than have anyone deprive me of this boast. Yet when I preach the gospel, I cannot boast, for I am compelled to preach. Woe to me if I do not preach the gospel! If I preach voluntarily, I have a reward; if not voluntarily, I am simply discharging the trust committed to me. What then is my reward? Just this: that in preaching the gospel I may offer it free of charge, and so not make use of my rights in preaching it.*

*Though I am free and belong to no man, I make myself a slave to everyone, to win as many as possible. To the Jews I became like a Jew, to win the Jews. To those under the law I became like one under the law (though I myself am not under the law), so as to win those under the law. To those not having the law I became like one not having the law (though I am not free from God's law but am under Christ's law), so as to win those not having the law. To the weak I became weak, to win the weak. I have become all things to all men so that by all possible means I might save some. I do all this for the sake of the gospel, that I may share in its blessings.*

*Do you not know that in a race all the runners run, but only one gets the prize? Run in such a way as to get the prize. Everyone who competes in the games goes into strict training. They do it to get a crown that will not last; but we do it to get a crown that will last forever. Therefore I do not run like a man running aimlessly; I do not fight like a man beating the air. No, I beat my body and make it my slave so that after I have preached to others, I myself will not be disqualified for the prize (I Corinthians 9:1-27).*

In chapter 8 Paul taught that believers cannot always follow their liberated consciences in such matters as eating meat dedicated to idols. They must also take into account the conscience scruples of their brothers and sisters in the congregation who do not have the same freedom that others may have. The chapter ends with a declaration by the apostle that he would rather become a vegetarian if meat should cause his brother to fall.

Chapter 9 is a kind of commentary on this attitude of Paul toward other people. He begins by listing a number of rights and privileges which he as an apostle might legitimately enjoy which, however, he gave up for the sake of others. The chapter closes with an illustration taken from the stadium and is a strong appeal to follow Paul's example. Chapter 9, in other words, shows that Paul practices what he preaches.

### I. Paul's Claim to Certain Rights (9:1-12a)

Paul begins with a series of rhetorical questions which call for an affirmative answer. He is a free man and that meant, among other things, that he was free from the dietary laws of Judaism and free to eat meat offered to idols.

Moreover, he is an apostle — something his Corinthian critics had put in doubt. Two arguments should settle this question: One, he had seen the risen Christ on the way to Damascus and that qualified him for apostleship. Two, the church at Corinth was established by him — "in the Lord," he humbly adds. The former is the foundation of apostleship, the latter a practical demonstration (v. 1).

Should others, to whom Paul was a stranger, call his apostleship in question they might be pardoned but the Corinthians should not raise this question for they are the proof (the seal, the stamp) of his apostolic calling (v. 2).

Evidently some Corinthians had questioned Paul's apostolicity on the grounds that he had claimed no privileges. He did not insist on eating what he pleased or eating at the church's expense. But he wants his readers to know that he had this right, only that he did not insist on it (vv. 3,4).

Talking about rights Paul mentions his freedom to be accompanied by a wife. No one would question Paul's right to marry but the apostle means more, namely, to be accompanied by a wife at the church's expense. There would be nothing very singular about such a privilege either for the Lord's brothers (who had become believers and were now faithful witnesses) did just that. Moreover, Peter, in his itinerant ministry, was accompanied by his wife (v. 5). Whether they had both been at Corinth on some occasion is not known. According to tradition, Peter's wife died a martyr's death together with her husband.

Some Corinthians evidently doubted the apostolicity of Paul because he earned his daily bread at his trade. (In Greece, free men, particularly those of the upper strata of society, did not normally engage in manual labor.) To put it differently, because Paul did not insist on a fee for his teaching some thought it couldn't be worth very much. (Church people today sometimes evaluate the worth of a speaker by the kind of honorarium he demands.)

Evidently Barnabas, Paul's companion on his first missionary journey, also thought nothing of working for his keep and Paul asks his readers whether he and Barnabas do not have the right to work if they so pleased.

There were occasions when Paul was happy to receive financial support from the churches, but evidently in his pioneer efforts at Corinth he deemed it wiser to work for his living and to preach the gospel gratis. This decision, however, should not be interpreted to mean that he did not have the right to be supported financially by the Corinthians (v. 6).

If in everyday life people enjoy the fruits of their labor why not in the realm of the spiritual? No soldier pays his own way when he goes to war for his country. He can expect food and clothing, if not a stipend.

Or take the fruit grower! Would he grow grapes and never eat any himself? Similarly, the man who tends a flock drinks of the milk of the flock. Everyone understands that in daily life people live by the labor of their hands (v. 7).

But the Scriptures also bear witness to this basic principle and so, besides the examples from ordinary life, Paul claims biblical warrant for his right to receive an honorarium for working at Corinth (v. 8).

In Deuteronomy 25:4 God prohibits an Israelite from muzzling the ox that treads out the grain (a primitive method of threshing which one can observe even today in the Near East). In this way the beast could also enjoy some of the fruit of its toil. (When a farmer today puts nose-guards on well fed horses he is not in violation of this human law.)

Paul's question: "Does God care for the oxen?" must be answered in the negative. His concern is not primarily with oxen but with his people, Israel; they are to learn to be kind to animals. Obviously, said Martin Luther, this law was not given for the sake of oxen since they cannot read anyway. So it must be a law given to the people of God. Moreover, the animal creation, according to Genesis 1:28, exists for man's benefit (v. 9).

This Old Testament regulation is now applied to the worker in God's field. "The plowman should plough in hope and the thresher threshes in hope of sharing in the crop" (v. 10). No farmer ploughs or threshes without hoping to gain from his labors. Similarly, those who sow spiritual seed are eligible to reap material reward (v. 11). And if others have this right, Paul, above all, had the right to be supported by the Corinthians. But he had not insisted on this right.

## II. Reasons for Waiving His Rights (9:12b-23)

(a) *Not to hinder the Gospel* (12b-14). Paul and his associates made the decision when they came to Corinth that they would support themselves. (In pioneer work the "tent-making" ministry has very much in its favor.) Paul did not want to put an obstacle in the way of the gospel. Instead, he was willing to endure privation and poverty for the sake of the kingdom (v. 26). If Paul had asked for financial support his missionary motives could easily have been misconstrued.

This is still a very important principle in the gospel ministry. God's servants should make sure there is nothing in their manner of life which hinders the communication of the Good News.

Just to remind his readers once more that he had the right to be supported by the church, he mentions the priests of the temple; they receive portions of what they sacrifice on the altar. Those employed in the temple get their food from the temple (v. 13).

However, not only is it true in everyday life and in the temple cult that a laborer is worthy of his hire, but our Lord also taught this principle. "Those who proclaim the gospel," said Jesus, "should get their living from the gospel." Whereas these exact words are nowhere found in our canonical gospels, Jesus said essentially what Paul has here, "the laborer deserves his wages" (Luke 10:17).

If our Lord did in fact give this command, why then did Paul not obey it when preaching in Corinth? Either Paul understood Jesus' words to mean that a laborer in God's field was permitted to receive wages, but need not insist on it, or else he took Jesus' words to be directed at the church and not at the worker. The church should take this word of Jesus seriously; the worker might well be reminded of another word of Jesus: "Freely you have received; freely give" (Mt. 10:8).

(b) *To have a ground for boasting* (15-18). Another reason Paul declined financial support while at Corinth was the deep satisfaction he got from proclaiming the Good News gratis.

It is hard for a preacher to talk to the church about money and Paul hopes his readers do not interpret what he has said about his right to be supported as a complaint about their past neglect. He would rather die, as he puts it, than to be deprived of the ground for boasting (v. 15). What he means by "boasting" he will explain presently.

He finds no such ground for boasting in the fact that he preaches the gospel for that is not optional in his case. He feels under compulsion to do that. Not to preach would mean to disobey the Lord who entrusted him with the gospel and made him a steward of the gospel. Refusal would have serious consequences (v. 16).

Paul is duty-bound to preach the gospel but he does not have to proclaim it gratis. Jesus called him to apostleship but Jesus did not say that Paul had to work without pay.

Therefore, he can't boast in the fact that he is a preacher; he was drafted into this service. But when he decides to serve without pay, he gets a deep sense of satisfaction out of that. This is the reward that he talks about (v. 17).

He asks: "What is my reward? Just this: that in my preaching I make the gospel free of charge" (v. 18). Whereas he had the authority to ask for financial support, he did not make "full use" of his right.

It should not be forgotten that Paul is addressing the question of whether the strong Corinthian has the right to live according to his understanding without regard to his weaker brother. Paul argues that for the sake of others we may have to sacrifice rights and privileges.

(c) *To save souls* (19-23). The overarching concern in Paul's life is the salvation of others. This concern to win people for Christ determines his lifestyle. Whereas he is a freeman, he makes himself a slave to all, so that he might win more people to Christ (v. 19).

In this language we hear an echo of Jesus' words in Mark 10:45, "The Son of man has come not to be served but to serve and to give his life a ransom for many." This decision to serve others does not conflict with Paul's warning (7:22, "don't become the slaves of men." When Paul serves others it is not because they have him under control; he remains Christ's "freedman." But out of love for souls he sacrifices his freedom to win others.

As an illustration of what this meant in daily life, he adds: "To the Jews I became as a Jew in order to win Jews" (v. 20). Paul was a Jew but he no longer felt bound to his Jewish past in such matters as dietary laws, circumcision, and the like. However, when he was with Jews he observed Jewish customs in order not to offend them. An example might be the circumcision of Timothy, designed to remove all cause of offence to Jews. He even made a Nazirite vow and respected Jewish festivals. Perhaps when he ate with Jews he observed their food laws. No doubt this is what he means when he says, "to those under the law I became as one under the law." By "law" here he may have had the 613 rabbinic precepts in mind.

Paul is quick to add that by adapting to Jewish laws he is not getting himself entangled in legalism. Jewish practices are neutral and indifferent, as far as he is concerned, and he respects these only for the purpose of winning those "under the law."

In the company of Gentiles, however, Paul takes a different approach. In order to win the non-Jews he disregards Jewish practices. To describe Gentiles as being "without law" does not mean that they are necessarily lawless, but rather, that they do not live by Jewish laws. In seeking to win people who have no roots in Judaism Paul also becomes "without law." And lest that be misconstrued to mean that the apostle compromises moral principles, he quickly adds: "not being without law toward God but under the law of Christ" (v. 21).

Some Christian workers in their desire to identify with people and to be "with it" sacrifice moral principles. When a young man tells me that he went to a dance in order to witness to a girl one doubts whether he is really "under the law of Christ." To be under the law of Christ is to follow Christ's example and to obey his teachings.

To the weak Paul becomes weak in order to win the weak (v. 22). Here probably those people with conscience scruples about things that were indifferent for Paul are in focus. Perhaps we have an allusion here to the problem of eating meat offered to idols. To sum it up Paul says: "I have become all things to all men, that I might by all means save some" (RSV).

This adaptability and flexibility probably appeared as icon

sistency to some observers. It is in fact consistent, robust Christianity. Paul's life-style was governed by his calling to win others for Christ. Modestly he confesses that he cannot save everybody, but he wants to save "some." Spurgeon, on one occasion, parodied Paul's words: "Some preachers are all things to all men so that they might win a *sum.*" That makes a sycophant, hardly a winner of souls.

So Paul restricts himself, sacrifices his liberties, for the sake of the gospel, "that I may share in its blessings" (v. 23). By putting restrictions on himself for the sake of others Paul's life is not impoverished but enriched. How rich are the lives of some of Christ's faithful servants who have sacrificed houses and lands for the sake of the kingdom! To Timothy, Paul wrote later: "By doing so you will save both yourself and your hearers" (I Tim. 4:16). In the process of trying to save others Timothy would (as did Paul) experience his own salvation at a deeper level.

### III. Illustrations of Voluntary Restrictions (9:24-27)

The Corinthians were familiar with athletic contests for every two years the Isthmian Games were played in the neighborhood of Corinth. Paul draws several illustrations from the sports arena to underscore the need for discipline and voluntary restrictions if one wants to win a prize.

All runners in the stadium run (*stadion* in Greek is 600 feet) but only one receives the prize (usually a wreath). Obviously Paul does not mean that Christians compete for a single prize which only the top spiritual athlete can obtain. Rather, Christians must discipline themselves if they are to win others for Christ and be rewarded on the last day. They must run according to the rules, one might say.

That this is the point of the illustration can be seen from verse 25: "Every athlete exercises self-control in all things." The word "athlete" here is the participle *agonizomenos* (struggling, wrestling, fighting). *Agon* to begin with was the race-track, then the struggle itself. Our derivative is "agony." The training of Greek athletes was at times nothing less than tyrannical, real agony.

They endured all this discipline and pain for the purpose of obtaining a perishable wreath. How much more should Christians exercise spiritual descipline in order to win others for Christ and in the end to receive Christ's "well done?" (v. 25).

We should not infer from Paul's use of these metaphors from the stadium that he was a sports fan. Even as a boy in Tarsus his parents, being orthodox Jews, would hardly have allowed him to attend the public games. Hellenistic society, however, was well familiar with the arena and so Paul frequently draws his figures of speech from this area.

Taking himself as example, Paul claims that he does not run aimlessly and he does not box as one beating the air. He lives his life on principle: he wants to win others, and for this Christ will reward him on the last day (v. 26).

In order to achieve this goal he puts restrictions on himself. Using a word from boxing, he says that he "pummels his body" — literally: "I give myself a black eye." Paul does not look upon his body as an enemy that must be subdued. "Body" is used in the sense of "person." Paul disciplines himself; he restricts himself with respect to things that are perfectly good and right as a safeguard for his own spiritual life. "Lest after preaching to others I myself should be disqualified" (v. 27).

The language of this final statement appears also to come from the arena. The verb "preach" is *kerusso,* and the noun *kerux* was used of the umpire at the games. How terrible, Paul seems to say, after laying down the rules for others, "calling the shots," to break the rules of the game and to sit in the penalty box.

In the homily known as *Second Clement* we read: "We must realize that if a contestant in a corruptible contest is caught cheating, he is flogged, removed and driven from the course. What do you think? What shall be done with a man who cheats in the contest of the incorruptible?" (7:4f.).

### Personal Response

1. *What, if any, rights do believers have? What, if any, rights do ministers have?*
2. *Paul asks several questions regarding the exercise of his rights (vv. 1-7). Under what circumstances is it appropriate for believers to exercise their rights?*
3. *Paul comments in verse 12 that he ". . . did not use this right." In what circumstances should believers give up their rights?*
4. *Why do people find it so difficult to give up their rights?*

# CHAPTER FOURTEEN

## The Danger of Indulgence

*For I do not want you to be ignorant of the fact, brothers, that our forefathers were all under the cloud and that they all passed through the sea. They were all baptized into Moses in the cloud and in the sea. They all ate the same spiritual food and drank the same spiritual drink; for they drank from the spiritual rock that accompanied them, and that rock was Christ. Nevertheless, God was not pleased with most of them; their bodies were scattered over the desert.*

*Now these things occurred as examples, to keep us from setting our hearts on evil things as they did. Do not be idolaters, as some of them were; as it is written: "The people sat down to eat and drink and got up to indulge in pagan revelry." We should not commit sexual immorality, as some of them did — and in one day twenty-three thousand of them died. We should not test the Lord, as some of them did — and were killed by snakes. And do not grumble, as some of them did — and were killed by the destroying angel.*

*These things happened to them as examples and were written down as warnings for us, on whom the fulfillment of the ages has come. So, if you think you are standing firm, be careful that you don't fall! No temptation has seized you except what is common to man. And God is faithful; he will not let you be tempted beyond what you can bear. But when you are tempted, he will also provide a way out so that you can stand up under it.*

97

> *Therefore, my dear friends, flee from idolatry. I speak to sensible people; judge for yourselves what I say. Is not the cup of thanksgiving for which we give thanks a participation in the blood of Christ? And is not the bread that we break a participation in the body of Christ? Because there is one loaf, we, who are many, are one body, for we all partake of the one loaf.*
>
> *Consider the people of Israel: Do not those who eat the sacrifices participate in the altar? Do I mean then that a sacrifice offered to an idol is anything, or that an idol is anything? No, but the sacrifices of pagans are offered to demons, not to God, and I do not want you to be participants with demons. You cannot drink the cup of the Lord and the cup of demons too; you cannot have a part in both the Lord's table and the table of demons. Are we trying to arouse the Lord's jealousy? Are we stronger than he? (I Corinthians 10:1-22).*

In chapter 8 Paul began to deal with the question of whether Christians had the freedom to eat meat offered to idols. In chapter 9 he digressed from this subject in order to demonstrate how he personally handled his Christian liberties. As a staunch monotheist Paul agreed with those Corinthians who put no stock in idols and, therefore, had no scruples about eating idol meat. However, the law of love does not permit believers who have this freedom to ride roughshod over the weak. They must be ready (as Paul was) to limit their freedoms for the sake of others.

Yet a further reason is now given for putting restrictions upon oneself. Eating food in idol temples constitutes a temptation to be ensnared by the powers of evil. Whereas it is right not to believe in idols, one should not underestimate the satanic powers at work in this evil system. That baptism and the Eucharist do not offer automatic protection against the evils of idolatry can be seen from Israel's history. And to that we now turn.

## I. The Privileges of God's People (10:1-4)

Paul begins by recounting the profound experiences of God's grace and power in Israel's early history. He will then show that in spite of all these blessings God's people fell into sin and suffered divine judgment as a consequence. This should serve as a warning to the overly confident Corinthians. What the athlete wins by discipline (9:24-27), Israel lost by indulgence.

What were some of Israel's great blessings? First, "our fathers were all under the cloud." It is instructive to note that Paul, writing to gentile Christians, speaks of old Israel as "our" fathers. The wild branches (the Gentiles) have been grafted into the Abrahamic tree, to use the language of Romans 11. And because there is a continuity between the old and the new Israel, the experiences of the people of the old covenant can serve as lessons for those of the new.

To be under the cloud does not mean to be in darkness or in sorrow, but means, rather, to be under divine protection and guidance. The reference is to the cloud by which God guided Israel when she left Egypt (a cloud which was fiery at night). It was the cloud that kept Pharaoh from capturing his runaway slaves, the Israelites. Israel could never forget this manifestation of divine grace at the time of the Exodus.

God's protecting care was experienced even more miraculously when Israel walked through the waters of the sea. This is described as a baptism into Moses (v. 2). In Exodus 14:31 we read that after they came safely through the sea they believed in God but also in Moses. He was now their accredited leader and they were now bound to him in trust and loyalty.

It is often overlooked in our baptismal theology that baptism upon confession of faith means to pledge one's loyalty to Christ. Years ago I attended a baptismal service in which the baptismal candidate (who was being baptized on confession of faith) was asked the question: "And do you promise to be true to Jesus until death?" A question like that adds depth to the baptismal liturgy.

In Judaism the passage through the Sea of Reeds, as the Hebrew has it, became the prototype for proselyte baptism since the making of the covenant (at Sinai) followed upon this "water baptism."

Israel's blessings, however, did not end with her deliverance out of Egypt. She also "ate spiritual food" (v. 3). The reference is to the manna, which was quite literally material food, but since it was supplied by God it was viewed as "supernatural" food, hence, spiritual. Obliquely there is a reference here to the bread that the Corinthians ate at the Eucharist. And just as eating manna did not keep Israel from sin, so the Lord's Supper will not keep the Corinthians from apostasy.

Not only was their food supplied supernaturally but they also drank "spiritual drink." The water from the rock was pure $H_2O$, but since it was supplied supernaturally Paul calls it spiritual drink. The allusion to the cup at the Lord's Table should not escape us. In a eucharistic prayer, found in the second century *Didache,* the writer speaks of the Lord's Supper as "spiritual food and drink" (v. 3).

Israel's supernatural blessings, Paul continues, had a christological source. "For they drank from the supernatural Rock which followed them, and the Rock was Christ" (v. 4). In the Pentateuchal narrative God supplied water from the rock both at the beginning (Ex. 17) and at the end of the journey (Num. 20) through the wilderness and so Jewish legend had it that the rock followed Israel for forty years and supplied them with water.

Paul does not endorse the legend but he uses it to teach the pre-existence of Christ. The Christ who came into the flesh when the time was fulfilled, and in whom the Corinthians trusted for their salvation, was also the One who supplied the needs of the Old Testament people of God.

But in spite of all these marvellous experiences of divine guidance, deliverance and sustenance, the old people of God fell away from the living God.

## II. The Failures of God's People (10:5-13)

"Nevertheless, with most of them God was not pleased; for they were overthrown in the wilderness" (v. 5). That is a deliberate understatement (called "meiosis") for in fact the entire generation of military age, twenty years and older when they left Egypt, was buried in the desert. They began with great spiritual blessings and ended up sowing the sand with corpses. And why? Because they took liberties from them that proved a snare; they indulged in idolatrous practices.

Such tragedies should serve as warnings for the new people of God so that they do not also become "lusters after evil" (v. 6). The word *tupoi* has various meanings: the mark of a blow, the stamp of a dye, a standard, a type. It can also mean an example for imitation or, as here, "warnings."

The examples of Israel's failure seem to be taken deliberately from her early history, her youth, and that makes their application to the young church at Corinth all the more apropos. Quite incidentally,

Paul shows us in this passage how the Old Testament may be used for instruction, warning and exhortation in the church.

Since Paul is dealing with the matter of eating meat offered to idols, it is not surprising that he points to Israel's propensity for falling into idolatry. Hence the warning: "Do not be idolators as some of them were" (v. 7). The most despicable lapse into idolatry in Israel's early history took place at Sinai where, after entering into covenant with Yahweh, they worshiped the golden bull-calf. The quotation, "The people sat down to eat and to drink and rose up to dance" (Ex. 32:6), is not only a reference to the tragedy at Sinai but is a kind of summary of what happened at idol feasts which some Corinthians evidently felt free to attend.

Closely associated with idol worship were immoral sexual practices and so Paul warns his readers against fornication (v. 8). Israel succumbed repeatedly to the immoral practices of the fertility cults but the event Paul has in mind in our passage is the tragedy at Peor where Israel played the harlot with the daughters of Moab (Num. 25). The sad consequence of Israel's immorality was the death of 23,000 people (Num. 25:9 puts it at 24,000).

Another catastrophe in Israel's history is the judgment of God by "fiery" serpents. The reason was that they put God to the test to see how far they could go (the application to the Corinthian situation is only too obvious).

Another besetting temptation of Israel was to grumble, which was a form of rebellion against God and his ways. As a result she was "destroyed by the Destroyer" (v. 10). Paul probably has the rebellion of Korah in mind (Num. 16), where the fire of Yahweh destroyed the rebels. Whereas the angel of the Lord is not mentioned in this Old Testament passage, he is viewed by Paul as the agent of God's wrath.

"All these things," says Paul by way of summary, "happened to them as a warning, but they were written down for our instruction" (v. 11). The Corinthians should learn from Israel's failure that a good beginning is no guarantee of a happy ending if one is not willing to put any restrictions on one's liberties. These tragic events were recorded, explains Paul, so that God's people would not forget them and could be instructed by them. The Corinthians lived in the days of fulfillment, "the ends of the ages" had come upon them (v. 11). However, as those who live in the new age, they must learn from the failures of the people of God of former ages.

Paul concludes his record of Israel's failure with a warning to the strong Corinthians not to be too brazen and cocky. "Therefore, let anyone who thinks he stands take heed lest he fall" (v. 12). It's a warning to those readers who felt free to go to the temples and eat idol meat because they no longer believed in idols. Such over-confidence could easily lead to temptation and sin. They should, therefore, restrict their liberties not only out of respect for the overly conscientious brethren, but also for the sake of their own spiritual good.

On the other hand, Paul does not want to frighten his readers, and so he adds a word of comfort (v. 13). Testings in themselves are not evil but are designed to bring out the true character of God's people. Temptations to immorality, idolatry, or other sins, are common to man. The Corinthians should, therefore, not complain that they were being tempted above their ability to endure.

Moreover, God is trustworthy and he will not expose them to temptation they cannot resist. In fact, with each temptation he will provide the way out so that they can endure it. One way of escape is to be wary of idolatrous practices. In the words of one divine, "God does not build walls around us so we cannot fall down the cliff; he builds wills within us so that we won't go too close to the brink."

### III. Warnings for God's People (10:14-22)

To be kept from falling into idolatrous practices demands that the Corinthians flee from idolatry. To "flee" is a figure of speech for avoidance. The language is reminiscent of Joseph's flight from the wife of Potiphar. Normally flight is thought of as a sign of defeat or cowardice, but to flee from idolatry is an expression of moral strength (v. 14).

To underscore his warning against the dangers of idolatry (even when one does not believe in idols) Paul will illustrate from the Lord's Supper and from Old Testament sacrifices that participation in a sacred meal puts one into fellowship with the God (or gods) at whose table one eats. As sensible people Paul expects them to grasp readily the force of his argument (v. 15).

(a) *Illustrations* (vv. 16-18). When believers at the Lord's Table drink of the cup over which a blessing has been spoken, they participate in the blood of Christ. The "cup of blessing" is a Jewish expression and was the third of the four cups drunk at the Passover meal, or the cup with which a meal ended. The *Didache* preserves a blessing spoken over the cup at the Lord's Table in the early church: "We give Thee thanks, our Father, for the holy vine of David Thy servant, which Thou hast made known to us through Jesus Thy Servant; Thine be the glory forever" (9:2).

Similarly, when the church partakes of the broken bread it participates in the body of Christ. Neither the "blood" nor the "body" of Christ has a material sense in our text but by partaking of the sacred elements the believer participates in the benefits of Christ's sacrificial death. (In Chapter eleven the cup/bread order is reversed. That shows the freedom with which the early church celebrated the Eucharist).

As an aside, Paul points out that the unity of the church is seen nowhere as clearly as at the Lord's Table. Eating of the same loaf the church, however many members, constitutes one body (v. 17).

Old Testament sacrifices illustrate the same point as the Christian Eucharist. "Look at Israel according to the flesh" (v. 18). This is earthly Israel with its temple cult. The church is the new Israel "according to the Spirit" (Gal. 4:29).

In the Levitical cult a portion of certain sacrifices was eaten by those who offered them; another portion was burnt on the altar. In this way the offerer shared in the altar. The altar was built for God and so the offerer, by eating of the sacrifice, came into fellowship with the God to whom the offering was brought.

(b) *Application* (vv. 19-22). If eating at the Lord's Table put one into fellowship with Christ and if eating of the sacrifice on the altar put one in touch with the God of the altar, then Paul's readers could draw only one conclusion: eating idol meat put a person into fellowship with the false gods.

At this point Paul anticipates strong objections from the strong Corinthians who held that the idol was a nonentity (8:4). Besides, Paul was guilty of a screaming contradiction, they must have thought. For in chapter 8 he agreed that the idol was nothing. Therefore, Paul quickly assures his readers that he does not believe in the reality of idols and so, in effect, does not believe in idol meat either (v. 19). His staunch monotheistic faith would not allow that.

It is not that he has changed his position on idols, but he

realizes that demonic forces are at work in idolatry (v. 20). There is an echo here of Deuteronomy 32:17: "They sacrificed to demons which were no gods." Feasts were under the patronage of pagan gods in Paul's day and those who shared in such feasts ate at the god's table, as it were. The real force behind all this idolatry was demons, and Paul does not want the Corinthians to have partnership with demons.

To participate in pagan practices involves the believer in a contradiction. "You cannot drink the cup of the Lord and the cup of demons. You cannot partake of the table of the Lord and the table of demons" (v. 21). At the risk of sounding hopelessly old-fashioned, this passage has been for me a constant deterrent against such things as the use of alcoholic beverages. Who can deny that alcohol is one of the greatest plagues on our society?

Paul concludes this section with one rhetorical question: "Shall we provoke the Lord to jealousy?" When Israel in the wilderness tried to combine the worship of the golden calf with the worship of Yahweh they stirred the Lord to jealousy (Deut. 32:17,21f.). A jealous God is one who wants the entire devotion of his people; divided loyalties call forth his judgment. And since we are not stronger than he (v. 22) we'd better not act with impunity, but humbly pray "lead us not into temptation, but deliver us from evil."

### *Personal Response*

1. *Paul opens this discussion with an example from Israel's history (vv. 1-5). What are the benefits of having examples, both positive and negative, to follow?*
2. *How can the church hold up positive models for youth to follow?*
3. *God will provide a way out of temptation (v. 13). What steps can believers take to overcome temptation?*
4. *What is the lure of temptation to sin? What are the steps into sin?*

# CHAPTER FIFTEEN

## When Things Aren't Black or White

*"Everything is permissible" — but not everything is beneficial.
"Everything is permissible" — but not everything is constructive.
Nobody should seek his own good, but the good of others.*

*Eat anything sold in the meat market without raising questions
of conscience, for, "The earth is the Lord's, and everything in it."*

*If some unbeliever invites you to a meal and you want to go, eat
whatever is put before you without raising questions of conscience.
But if anyone says to you, "This has been offered in sacrifice," then
do not eat it, both for the sake of the man who told you and for conscience's sake — the other man's conscience, I mean, not yours. For
why should my freedom be judged by another's conscience? If I take
part in the meal with thankfulness, why am I denounced because
of something I thank God for?*

*So whether you eat or drink or whatever you do, do it all for
the glory of God. Do not cause anyone to stumble, whether Jews,
Greeks or the church of God — even as I try to please everybody
in every way. For I am not seeking my own good but the good of
many, so that they may be saved. Follow my example, as I follow
the example of Christ (I Corinthians 10:23-11:1).*

In this paragraph Paul brings together the threads of his
arguments on the subject of eating meat offered to idols. He has just
warned his readers (10:14-22) against participation in idol festivals,

for they would be exposing themselves to sinister powers, dangerous to their spiritual life.

However, when it comes to purchasing meat for home consumption, believers should not let it bother them that the meat may have been dedicated to idols. Also, they should not be overly fussy about foods when invited by an unbelieving friend for dinner, unless someone pointed out the sacrificial origin of the meat on the table.

On the surface all of this seems to be irrelevant to Bible readers in the Western world. Quite the opposite, however, is the case! Paul lays down guidelines for Christian conduct that can be applied in a great many life-situations, even in our day. In fact, the following paragraph is a rich source of instruction in the area of ethical decision-making.

In the realm of ethics we often face situations which are neither black nor white, where we cannot say that this or that is clearly right or wrong. There are, of course, plenty of moral absolutes in the Scriptures. Murder, fornication, greed, envy, and the like, are always wrong. But we all know of hundreds of practices in our day that are clearly ambivalent; they lie in the area of the grays. Ethicists call them adiaphora (*diaphoros* in Greek means "different"; adiaphora means things which are "indifferent," they are neither right nor wrong in themselves).

Paul begins this summary paragraph with a few general guidelines for Christian conduct.

## I. General Guidelines (10:23,24)

"All things are lawful" seems to have been a libertarian slogan in Corinth and Paul has quoted it on an earlier occasion (6:12). Asssuming for the moment that a Corinthian had the freedom to have a meal with his friends in an idol temple, without conscience qualms, does this give him the right to do so? Paul adds a qualifying condition: It may be lawful but "not all things are helpful." (The verb "to be helpful" (*sumphero* — to bring together) can also be translated "to be profitable," "to be expedient.")

There may be many indifferent things which a believer might do with a good conscience but which are not helpful in his spiritual growth. Jonathan Goforth spoke of them as "leakages of power," even though not wrong in themselves. Some things good in themselves cost an awful lot of money and absorb an inordinate amount of time. Are they really helpful?

Once again Paul quotes the slogan of the liberated Corinthian, "all things are lawful" and adds a second qualification, "but not all things build up" (v. 23). There are many things in our culture which one could not label as sin, but which, instead of contributing to our spiritual growth, lower our ideals, blunt our consciences and rob us of our moral fortitude. When something harms our body, our mind, our inner life, Paul would counsel us to desist and to seek rather those things which are for our benefit.

A third general guideline is: the good of our neighbor (v. 24). This is the law of love which was manifested by our Lord, of whom Paul says that "he pleased not himself" (Rom. 15:3). To the Philippians he wrote: "Let each of you look not to his own interests, but also to the interests of others," and then shows that this was the mind of Christ. The loving consideration of others and the promotion of their highest good is a fundamental rule in a believer's use of his liberties.

Following these three general guidelines for adiaphorous situations, Paul gets down to specifics.

### II. Specific Instructions (10:25-30)

(a) *For those eating at home* (vv. 25,26). Those Corinthians who go to the market (KJV reads "shambles" — an archaic word for tables on which meat was placed in the open market) to buy their meat should not ask the seller how the animal was slaughtered, whether the meat was dedicated to some pagan god or the like. If they did they would constantly burden their consciences (v. 25). Observant Jews normally had their own orthodox slaughterer and would avoid purchasing meat at the public market. Gentile Christians hardly had this option. (Whether Jewish Christians had is hard to say.)

Interestingly, Paul does not insist on the Jerusalem decree which asked gentile Christians to abstain from what was sacrificed to idols (Acts 15:29). Paul counsels his readers to ask no questions when they buy a joint of meat at the market. For even if the one who slaughtered the animal had dedicated it to the gods, the believer need not eat it as idol meat. Here we see how completely Paul had been liberated from the dietary laws of his Jewish past.

In his fight against false asceticism Paul writes to Timothy, "Everything created by God is good and nothing is to be rejected if it is received with thanksgiving" (I Tim. 4:34). In our passage Paul says something very similar: "The earth is the Lord's and the fulness of it." This is a quotation from Psalm 24:1, and this passage was understood in Judaism to give the reason for saying grace at table. (When the writer was at seminary his Old Testament professor on one occasion prayed Psalm 24:1 before a meal — he did it in Hebrew.)

The implication is that a believer views the food he buys at the public market as God's gift to him, and that calls not for asking questions on how the food was produced, but rather for a glad thanksgiving to God the Giver of all food.

(b) *For those dining with unbelievers* (vv. 27-30). To some believers in our day Paul seems rather "worldly" at this point. Evidently he had no compunctions about eating with unbelievers and counsels his readers, if they are invited by unbelieving friends, to accept the invitation if they wish. It may be helpful to recall that Jesus used to eat with publicans and sinners (even with Simon, the Pharisee).

At the dining table of unbelievers Christians should make it a rule of thumb to eat whatever is served. When Jesus sent out the Seventy he told them to "eat what is set before you" (Lk. 19:8). Imagine how difficult this would be for a Christian Jew in the home of a gentile friend! It had taken a lot of persuading to get Peter to go to the home of Cornelius (Acts 10). Even between Jewish and gentile Christians table fellowship was a problematic question.

When dining at the table of an unbelieving host Christians should not ask questions about the food. However, it could happen that someone at the table might point out to the Christian guest that the meat on the table was temple meat. Who would do this kind of thing is not stated (the host? a fellow guest?). In any case, the Christian guest should then not eat the meat out of consideration for the one who pointed it out to him and for the sake of the other person's conscience. Perhaps the conscience of a Christian fellow guest is meant.

Here again we see that personal liberties must be kept within limits by the law of love; for by deliberately eating temple meat the strong believer would encourage the one with scruples to violate his conscience.

F.F. Bruce suggests a modern analogy. If someone with strong convictions on total abstention from alcohol were guest of friends who did not share his principles, he would be well advised not to inquire too carefully about the ingredients of some palatable sauce, let us say. If, however, someone said pointedly, "There's alcohol in this," he might feel that he is being put to the test and could then kindly ask to be excused from having it. But someone will object by asking: "Why should my liberty be determined by another man's scruples?" This is the kind of question a person who chafes under the narrowness of a fellow believer could ask. Or is it Paul asking rhetorically: "Why should I have my freedom in Christ criticized by a weaker brother? I will rather not eat, and then there's no criticism." Or is Paul saying, if someone refused to eat meat out of respect for another person's conscience, he should not fear that he is losing his freedom in Christ. It would much rather be a sign of his maturity.

Furthermore, the strong Christian, who is asked to give up his rights for the sake of a weaker brother, might legitimately complain; "I thanked God for this food; surely my brother can't denounce me now for eating it, even if it was purchased in the temple." Again it could be Paul asking: "Why incur blame for food for which you have thanked? Don't eat; then no one can accuse you."

Quite incidentally it is suggested here that Christians thank God for their food even in the home of an unbelieving friend (not with a display of piety, but perhaps with a silent prayer). Also, there is an implicit suggestion here that that for which we can give thanks is good and right.

### III. Abiding Principles (10:31,32)
"Whether you eat or drink, or whatever you do, do all to the glory of God" (v. 31). This is to be the overriding concern of the follower of Jesus.

In order to live for the glory of God one must of course know what glorifies him. This we can learn from the Scriptures. Horatius Bonar, the Scottish divine, writes: "I love my Master,...and I want to do His bidding, but I must know the rules of His house, that I may know how to serve Him." The question then is not simply whether this or the other thing is right or wrong, but whether it glorifies God. Those who are constantly debating about whether something is right or wrong operate at an elementary level; those who ask: "Will I glorify God if I do or not do something," operate at a higher level.

A second abiding principle for Christian ethics is spelled out in verse 32, "Give no offence to Jews or to Greeks or to the church of God." We have explained earlier that we offend others by encouraging them to act contrary to their conscience. In this way we cause them to stumble and to fall in their Christian life. This we must avoid at all cost.

The Jew and the Greek probably refer to the unbelieving community in contrast to the church of God. If this is so then Paul is warning us not to offend unbelievers by our manner of life and in this way keep them from embracing the Christian faith.

As so often, Paul points to himself as an example. This does not arise out of pride but out of the need to give these young Christians good models which they did not yet have.

### IV. Personal Example (10:33, 11:1)

Paul claims that he seeks to please all people in everything he does. This should not be understood as a contradiction of what he wrote to the Galatians: "If I were still pleasing men, I should not be a servant of Christ" (1:10). The apostle would never trim the truth of the gospel to make it more acceptable but he would do all in his power to make himself acceptable. He would avoid offending people or doing things that were in bad taste.

Lest the readers misunderstand Paul's concern to make himself acceptable to others he adds: "Not seeking my own advantage but that of the many, that they may be saved." Paul wants to remove all barriers that keep people from experiencing salvation. While it will not excuse the unbeliever in the final judgment, it is most disconcerting for a soul-winner to discover that an unbeliever is rejecting the Christian faith because of some misdemeanor, some raw deal, some hurtful word or deed of a professing Christian.

The first verse of chapter 11 seems to belong to chapter 10 (there were no such divisions in the original letter). Paul concludes his long discussion of Christian liberty by calling the Corinthians to become his followers. "Become imitators of me"! And lest that sound too pompous, he quickly adds: "as I am of Christ." Christ made himself the servant of all; Christ did not please himself;

Christ wanted only the good of others. These traits Paul had learned from his Master and he calls us to imitate him in these matters.

It may be in place to conclude this lengthy discussion by pulling together some of the abiding principles in ethical decision-making that seem to emerge from these chapters. When facing ambivalent situations one might ask questions such as these: (i) Will this be for my good? (ii) Will this contribute to my Christian growth? (iii) Can I thank God for what I am about to do? (iv) Will it glorify God? (v) Am I identifying with an evil system? (vi) Will I be a good example to my fellow Christians? (vii) Will it hinder or help in winning others for Christ?

When such questions are asked under the guidance of the Holy Spirit and in the light of the Word of God, we can more easily find our way through the tangled maze that life in a society such as ours at times seems to be.

### *Personal Response*

1. *Paul indicates that some people will think something is sin while other believers find it quite acceptable (vv. 27-28). List some actions which some people consider sin and others consider acceptable behavior. How do you feel about each of these? How do you decide whether to put each item into the "sin" or "not sin" column?*
2. *Are there times when one item might be sin and at other times when the same action might not be a sin (vv. 23-24)? Explain your answer.*
3. *Two believers are members of the same congregation. One believes that a certain practice is sin. The other finds liberty in engaging in the practice. How can these two remain in the same congregation and continue to love each other?*
4. *List principles which help you make ethical decisions.*

# CHAPTER SIXTEEN

## Head Covering for Women

*I praise you for remembering me in everything and for holding to the teachings, just as I passed them on to you.*

*Now I want you to realize that the head of every man is Christ, and the head of the woman is man, and the head of Christ is God. Every man who prays or prophesies with his head covered dishonors his head. And every woman who prays or prophesies with her head uncovered dishonors her head — it is just as though her head were shaved. If a woman does not cover her head, she should have her hair cut off; and if it is a disgrace for a woman to have her hair cut or shaved off, she should cover her head. A man ought not to cover his head, since he is the image and glory of God; but the woman is the glory of man. For man did not come from woman, but woman from man; neither was man created for woman, but woman for man. For this reason, and because of the angels, the woman ought to have a sign of authority on her head.*

*In the Lord, however, woman is not independent of man, nor is man independent of woman. For as woman came from man, so also man is born of woman. But everything comes from God. Judge for yourselves: Is it proper for a woman to pray to God with her head uncovered? Does not the very nature of things teach you that if a man has long hair, it is a disgrace to him, but that if a woman has long hair, it is her glory? For long hair is given to her as a covering. If anyone wants to be contentious about this, we have no*

113

> *other practice — nor do the churches of God (I Corinthians*
> *11:2-16).*

The following chapter does not appear to have been written in response to questions asked by the Corinthians. Chapter 11 deals with disorders in public worship — a problem to which the next four chapters (11-14) are devoted.

There were three areas in which the public worship in the Corinthian church left something to be desired: (i) the deportment of women, (ii) the manner of celebrating the Eucharist, and (iii) the use of spiritual gifts. Paul addresses these three problems in turn, beginning with the veiling of women.

Before he begins to criticize the apostle tactfully condemns the readers for remembering him and the "traditions" which he had taught them. The word "tradition" (*paradosis* — that which is handed down) is a bad word for people who belong to the "now" generation. In the gospels tradition is in fact a negative term, for there it often refers to the Jewish traditions which had so cluttered up the Word of God that people could no longer hear that Word. In the epistles, however, it stands for apostolic teaching (which went back to Jesus), whether oral or written. It is a word which indicates that the apostles did not develop their own theology independently of each other, but that they all drew from the same source: the gospel of Jesus Christ.

The Corinthians had sought to hold fast the traditions Paul had passed on to them. In other words, they tried to live by his teaching. That this was so can be seen also from the fact that they wrote to Paul and asked him questions about certain aspects of the Christian life. They wanted to conform to his instructions and for this he commends them.

There were, however, several areas of conduct in which Paul could not praise them. One of these was the behavior of some Corinthian women who violated the public sense of decency by refusing to wear the traditional headgear to church.

It may well be that they were carrying Paul's teaching, that in Christ there is neither male nor female, too far. Throughout the Near East women commonly covered their heads in public with a kerchief or small shawl. This was not a liturgical veil (and not a Moslem veil, either), but it belonged to the every day dress of decent women. By refusing to wear this traditional form of dress to church Corinthian women tended to bring the gospel into disgrace in their community. Paul, always concerned that the church have a good reputation in society, now gives his theological reasons why the distinction between men and women should be seen in the way they dressed.

### I. The Relationship of Male and Female (11:3-6)

(a) *The Meaning of Headship* (v. 3). Paul wants his readers to understand that "the head of every man is Christ, the head of a woman is her husband, and the head of Christ is God" (v. 3). Some think that "head" in this passage is used in the sense of "source" or "origin" (a meaning the word *kephale* certainly can have). Just as Christ comes from God and man (the male) comes from Christ, so the woman comes from man (in creation).

However, the word "head" is also used in the sense of "leader," and it appears to me this sense is not absent here. As Christ in his incarnation submitted to God, and man is subject to Christ (that the woman is also subject to Christ is thereby not denied), so the married woman is subject to her husband.

Feminists today object to this kind of language but it's the language of the Bible. Headship and submission, however, are never understood in terms of superiority and inferiority but refer rather to divinely assigned roles, each with its dignity and honor. Nor does headship mean that the husband has the right to lord it over his wife. Christ established his headship over the church (Eph. 5) by giving himself for her (not by force) and so the husband's headship over his wife cannot be divorced from his sacrificial love for her.

(b) *The Expression of Headship* (vv. 4-6). A man dishonors his head when he prays or prophecies in church with his head covered (v. 4). That not every man (or woman) has the gift of prophecy is a question left out of consideration at this point. Paul's concern here is that the man should participate in public worship with his head uncovered. There is no evidence that men were failing in this but the contrast is designed to underscore the neglect of the women (whether men in Jewish synagogues at this time wore the yarmulke or not is not certain, nor does it matter, since Paul is speaking of a veil and not a skull-cap.) So the man is to worship with an "unveiled face."

The woman (i.e. the wife), on the other hand, who prays and prophecies (she participates in worship fully with the man) and doesn't cover her head, dishonors it (v. 5). While the word "head" in verses 4 and 5 refers to the heads of man and woman respectively, there is probably an oblique reference in it to Christ, who is dishonored when the distinction between male and female is not observed.

Since it was a disgrace, by general consent, if a married woman appeared in public without her head covering, to do so in church was equally disgraceful. In fact, by doing so, she put herself on the level of the woman who has a shaved head. Whether Paul had pagan priestesses in mind, or the adulterous woman (Num. 5:18), or simply a woman of loose morals, is not stated (or does he mean simply that she then looks like a man?), but all decent Corinthian women would revolt at being placed in the category of the shaven women.

Paul seems to be telling the Corinthian women who discarded the traditional headcovering that if they take the first step out of bravado they may have begun the moral slide downwards. Verse 6 appears to bear this out. "For if a woman will not veil herself, then she should cut off her hair; but if it is disgraceful for a woman to be shorn or shaven, let her wear a veil." The Christian women of Corinth wouldn't think of shearing their hair. But Paul is suggesting that to disregard the veil puts them on the track that leads to shame and dishonor. Since it is not the custom for women in our society to cover their heads in public there is no need for them to do so in church either. Every society, however, has ways of distinguishing male and female by the way they dress. Unisex clothing, therefore, should be rejected by Christians. The distinction between male and female is not simply a matter of custom or convention, but has deep roots in creation.

## II. The Creation of Male and Female (11:7-12)

(a) *The Creation Order* (vv. 7-9). "A man ought not to cover his head for he is in the image and glory of God" (v. 7). This is a reference to the creation account in which the word "man" ( adam) is used in the generic sense, including the woman. Paul does not deny that the woman also was made in the image of God, but his concern in this passage is to show her relation to her husband. He does not say that Eve was made in Adam's image, but she is "the glory of man."

When God created man, he made Adam first and from him he made Eve (Gen. 2). Nor was the man created for the sake of the woman, but rather the women was created to be man's counterpart, "a helper fit for him" (Gen. 2:18,20). Man was made directly by God and reflects His glory; woman was made for man, and reflects *his* glory. Both have a dignity given to them by the Creator. They retain this dignity by respecting male and female distinctions.

It is often argued today, on the grounds of Galatians 3:28, where it is stated that in Christ there is neither male nor female, that the order of creation has been transcended by the order of redemption. However, while redemption undoes the affects of sin on marriage, it does not annul the creation order. F.F. Bruce comments: "Even if the order of the old creation has been transcended in Christ by the order of the new creation, yet, as long as the former order survives, those who are in Christ must show respect for it by their appearance and demeanor" (*I and II Cor.* (NCB), p. 105).

(b) *The Symbol of Dignity for the Woman* (v. 10). "This is why a woman ought to have a veil upon her head, because of the angels" (v. 10). This verse presents two major problems of translation and interpretation. Literally the text says that the woman should have "authority" *(exousia)* on her head (although a variant reading gives it as "veil" and Origen has "veil and authority"). Yet we expected Paul to say the opposite, namely that she should be in submission to authority and wear the head covering as a symbol of her submission.

Some have suggested that *exousia* be rendered as "dignity" for in that culture (as in ours) a woman properly dressed (i.e. with a head covering in Paul's day) could move about freely with dignity and respect.

"Morna Hooker has argued that we read the word *exousia* as "authority" but that the reference is to the woman's authority to pray and to prophecy in church (an authority she did not have in the synagogue) (NTS 10 (1963-64), pp. 410ff.).

Perhaps these various meanings are not as disparate as they appear. If the veil was a symbol of a married woman's submission to her husband, the wearing of it gave her full authority in her sphere as woman, but also it gave her dignity and security.

But what does "because of the angels" mean? Let me give several lines of interpretation and then suggest one which seems to us to be the correct one.

(1) Since angels are present when the church worships, women should observe the rules of propriety in the presence of these representatives of heaven. (That angels do observe our conduct is stated in Luke 15:7,10.)

(2) If women are not properly dressed they will tempt angels. According to one understanding of Genesis 6:1-4, angels were captivated by the beauty of the "daughters of men" in the early stages of mankind's history. This view hardly seems to fit I Corinthians 11.

(3) Since angels themselves veil their faces in the presence of God (Isa. 6;2), how much more should womenfolk cover their heads. This, too, is unlikely to be the meaning here.

(4) In Revelation 2 and 3 the leaders of the churches are called "angels" and if that were the meaning here (again, quite unlikely) Paul would be exhorting women to dress appropriately out of respect for the leaders of the church.

(5) Angels, in Jewish thought, were the guardians of this created order, and since Paul is dealing with the creation order, this is more likely to have been in his mind (So Bruce, Caird and others), although it is not thereby denied that angels are present when the church gathers for worship.

(c) *Complementarity in Christ* (vv. 11,12). This parenthesis is slipped in to offset the possibility of making the inference that the woman is inferior to the man. "In the Lord woman is not independent of man nor man of woman" (v. 11). Husband and wife are mutually interdependent; they complement each other. This would be true all the more if they are "in the Lord."

Although it is true that the first woman was made from man, since then every man has come from a woman (v. 12). And one cannot claim to have greater dignity than the other, since both of them (indeed "all things") are from God.

Whereas they are one in Christ, and complement one another in their marriage relationship, it is only proper that the distinction between male and female be observed. One way of observing it (in Paul's day) was for the woman to wear the customary head covering.

### III. Propriety for Male and Female (11:13-16)

(a) *The Voice of "nature"* (vv. 13-15). Paul appeals to his readers to follow his instructions on the basis of humanity's sense of propriety which "nature" itself instills.

Different cultures may have different concepts as to what is natural but as a general statement Paul's observation is true. (To use this passage to fix the precise length of a woman's hair or the shortness of a man's is hardly legitimate. However, just as the difference between male and female is seen in dress, so the difference should be visible in the length of hair. It is dishonoring to the Creator if men wear their hair as long as that of women. Although hair styles differ from culture to culture, and from time to time, there is a law written deeply into mankind, that men and women should wear their hair differently one from the other.)

The word "nature" (*phusis*) is used here much in the sense of "custom." A man with long hair was regarded as effeminate in Paul's day, whereas a woman's hair was regarded as her pride. "For her hair is given to her for a covering" (v. 15).

At first blush one wonders why Paul went to all the trouble arguing for a cloth head covering when in the end "he concedes that a woman's hair is given to her for a covering. Here we should not read the preposition (*anti*) to mean "in the place of"; rather, her hair covering is similar to the cloth covering. Since nature itself indicates that a woman's head should be covered by providing her with long hair, she should also wear a veil. If she refuses to wear her kerchief, then (so Paul argued above) let her also crop her hair. Her head of hair stands in harmony with her cloth covering dictated by convention.

(b) *The Practice of the Churches* (v. 16). Paul anticipates protest from some Corinthian women and so he reminds those who will be tempted to be contentious and disregard Paul's teachings on this matter that the churches of God recognize no other practice than the one he has just outlined.

There may have been a tendency for Corinth to be a law unto itself (a besetting temptation of large churches) but Paul wanted the churches to have a similar "face" in the Mediterranean world. He recognized (as many Christians today do not) that where there is unity in doctrine and ethics among the various churches, their witness to the unbelievers is immeasurably strengthened. We should not be surprised when unbelievers at times get utterly confused about Christianity, when churches have so little in common. While it may be too much to expect that all denominations agree in all matters of doctrine and ethics, surely one might expect a single denomination to be agreed on a core of doctrinal and ethical teachings.

Having followed Paul's argument in this passage, some readers today may still be asking: How much of this is applicable to the life of the church today? Before we mention a few items, let us remember that God's Word, while it is permanently applicable, was given in different cultural settings. And so we must constantly ask what it means to be obedient today to a word spoken in a different situation 2000 years ago.

Let me suggest the following:

(1) Christians should respect accepted social conventions. There are, of course, sinful social customs in society (also in the matter of dress) which believers will shun, but the Christian cause is not strengthened when that which is considered decent is flouted. Disregard for a given culture's social decorum does not add to the church's reputation. (Church members who get satisfaction out of flouting a church's customs might also take note.)

(2) The difference between male and female, as this expresses itself in different dress and hair style, should be observed. Men should not wear women's clothes and women not men's (and I don't mean that ladies' slacks are men's clothes). The Creator made the two sexes different and we should honor the creator by expressing that difference in dress and hair style.

(3) Propriety in dress should be observed at all times, but particularly when the church gathers for worship. When we gather in the presence of God we have more serious things to think about than the latest fashions (museum pieces are, of course, out of place too; they also attract attention). As we entered a cathedral in Prague two summers ago, a lady was asked to leave the church because, as she was told, she was not properly dressed. (4) Quite aside from the matter of dress, our passage gives women their rightful place in the worship of the church. If otherwise they respect social decorum, there is nothing in this passage that restricts them from participating fully in the worship services of God's people. That

freedom was given to the woman by the gospel. She is not to abuse this freedom but to use it for her own enrichment and the blessing of others.

### Personal Response

1. *Paul writes about the relationship between men and women. What is the relationship between male and female? What is the meaning of headship in verse three? What is the basis of the relationship between male and female (vv. 7-9)?*
2. *How is the biblical relationship between male and female reflected or not reflected in society today?*
3. *The head covering appears to be a cultural sign of the authority of men over women. How far should we go in following social customs in dress and behavior? Or in other matters of principle?*
4. *What is the role of women and men in worship?*

# CHAPTER SEVENTEEN

## The Lord's Supper

*In the following directives I have no praise for you, for your meetings do more harm than good. In the first place, I hear that when you come together as a church, there are divisions among you, and to some extent I believe it. No doubt there have to be differences among you to show which of you have God's approval. When you come together, it is not the Lord's Supper you eat, for as you eat, each of you goes ahead without waiting for anybody else. One remains hungry, another gets drunk. Don't you have homes to eat and drink in? Or do you despise the church of God and humiliate those who have nothing? What shall I say to you? Shall I praise you for this? Certainly not!*

*For I received from the Lord what I also passed on to you: The Lord Jesus, on the night he was betrayed, took bread, and when he had given thanks, he broke it and said, "This is my body, which is for you; do this in remembrance of me." In the same way, after supper he took the cup, saying, "This cup is the new covenant in my blood; do this, whenever you drink it, in remembrance of me." For whenever you eat this bread and drink this cup, you proclaim the Lord's death until he comes.*

*Therefore, whoever eats the bread or drinks the cup of the Lord in an unworthy manner will be guilty of sinning against the body and blood of the Lord. A man ought to examine himself before he eats of the bread and drinks of the cup. For anyone who eats and drinks without recognizing the body of the Lord eats and drinks judgment on himself. That is why many among you are weak and sick, and a number of you have fallen asleep. But if we judged ourselves, we would not come under judgment. When we are judged by the Lord, we are being disciplined so that we will not be condemned with the world.*

*So then, my brothers, when you come together to eat, wait for each other. If anyone is hungry, he should eat at home, so that when you meet together it may not result in judgment.*

*And when I come I will give further directions (I Corinthians 11:17-34).*

At the beginning of chapter 11 Paul commended his readers for keeping the "traditions" (i.e., teachings) which he had given them. His praise, however, is not unqualified. First, he had to criticize some Corinthian women who were taking their liberty in Christ too far and were offending against the public sense of decency by participating in worship without the conventional head covering. Paul states explicitly that he cannot praise them for this violation of the rules of propriety.

Moreover, there is a second matter for which he cannot praise them — something even more serious than the neglect of the head covering — namely, for the way the Lord's Supper is being celebrated. Assembling at the Lord's Table does them more harm than good (v. 17). What was intended for their spiritual benefit led to misconduct and consequent suffering.

This is, then, the second problem in public worship that Paul deals with in this letter. Let us seek to follow his thinking on this matter!

## I. Disorders at the Lord's Table (11:17-22)

"In the first place," says Paul (there is no "second," unless perhaps "the other things" in verse 34 are meant), "when you assemble as a church, I hear that there are divisions among you" (v. 18).

The word "church" (*ekklesia*) can refer to all the people of God in Christ, or to the believers in a local community, or, as in our text, to the actual "assembling" of the church on the first day of the week (but it never means a church building in the New Testament). According to Romans 16:23 the Corinthian church met in the house of Gaius.

At these meetings of the church, where the Lord's death was remembered by the bread and the cup, the divisions in the church became glaringly obvious. The divisions Paul refers to at this point are possibly not those for which he had criticized the Corinthians in chapters 1-4. Not party-strife but discrimination against the poor marred the fellowship of the saints at the Lord's Table.

Again and again Paul had heard about dissensions in the church and he believes what he has heard, but only "in part." That is a loving touch. He refuses to believe all the bad things he hears. "Love hopes all things" (I Cor. 13:7) — hopes it won't all be true. Perhaps we can take a hint from Paul here. When we hear evil rumors about a person or a church, we ought, as a rule, to believe only the half of what we hear.

Paul is realistic enough to expect factions in a church in which the members come from diverse backgrounds. Justin Martyr knew of a saying of Jesus (whether genuine or not, we do not know), which resembles what Paul says here: "There will be divisions and factions" (Dialogue 35.3). Divisions are always bad, but since they do arise (human nature being what it is), Paul sees some possible good emerging from them: "that those who are genuine among you may be recognized" (v. 19).

How does this happen? Perhaps by mediating and reconciling the factions the genuine saints come to the fore (*dokimoi* signifies that they have been put to the test and are now approved). Or perhaps by refusing to get caught in the fray, the genuine become manifest. Could it be that Paul has the final judgment in mind where the distinction between the genuine and the counterfeit will become manifest?

In any case, the factions in the Corinthian church make their gathering for the Lord's Supper a caricature of Christian fellowship. The fellowship meal at which the unity of the church is to be most visible (I Cor. 10:16,17) had degenerated into an ugly demonstration of selfishness.

This is the only text in which the Eucharist is called "the Lord's Supper." The adjective *kuriakos* (lordly, belonging to the Lord) is a word found in the secular papyri for "that which belongs to Caesar," "imperial" (as, for example, the "imperial" treasury). This adjective is found only here and in Revelation 1:10 where it describes the Christian Sunday as "the Lord's day."

That it should be called a "supper" should not surprise us since it was instituted at the passah meal just before our Lord's death, and this meal had to be eaten in the evening (in commemoration of the Exodus, which took place at night). Also, it should be underscored that the Eucharist, to begin with, was a regular meal at which Christ's death was remembered and not a token meal as churches generally practice it today.

To eat together is a symbol of fellowship (this is even more so in the Middle East). Eating together as a church today (quite aside from the Eucharist) is also subject to abuse but, as Edward Schweizer puts it, a church that doesn't eat hot-dogs together probably doesn't eat the Eucharist either. In other words, if the members of a congregation are so far removed from one another that they never participate in fellowship meals, then they are probably quite distant from each other even though they sit on the same pew at the Eucharist.

In Corinth the members of the church ordinarily brought their food and shared it at a communal meal. This would also provide the poor of the congregation with an opportunity to get a square meal. Because of the rifts in the church, however, individual Corinthians or groups brought their supper to church and ate it by themselves so that the rich had more than enough and the poor were left not only hungry, but humiliated (v.21). Whereas the class distinctions were to disappear at the Lord's Supper, in Corinth these distinctions between rich and poor became poignantly obvious at the Lord's Table. That kind of meal, where every one goes ahead with his own supper, says Paul, can hardly be called the Lord's Supper (v. 21). In fact, if they insisted on hiving themselves off from others during the supper they might as well be eating at home. Such conduct was an insult to the church and such unbrotherly behavior deserves no praise but only condemnation (v. 22).

## II. The Institution of the Lord's Supper (11:23-26)

This is the earliest recorded account of the institution of the Lord's Supper since the gospels were not yet published. However, there was a trustworthy oral tradition that went back to Jesus. Paul indicates this with the words, "For I received from the Lord what also I delivered to you" (v. 23). This is not a reference to direct revelation for the words "receive" and "deliver" are standard terms for the transmission of apostolic tradition. The oral tradition came to Paul through faithful witnesses but stems, ultimately, from the Lord himself.

To correct the Corinthian abuses Paul rehearses for them the account of the institution of the Lord's Supper. On the night when Jesus was betrayed, he took bread, "and when he had given thanks, he broke it, and said, "This is my body which is for you. Do this in remembrance of me" (vv. 24,25). Whereas the word rendered as "betrayed" refers to the treachery of Judas, the same word is used of Jesus being "delivered up for our trespasses" (Rom. 4:25) and this nuance may not be absent even in our text. After Judas has been given his full blame for betraying his Master, we should remember that Jesus was "delivered up according to the definite plan and foreknowledge of God" (Acts 2:23).

On this awful night of his betrayal Jesus had gathered with his disciples in the Upper Room and, as the Jewish *pater familias* at the Passover meal, he took the bread and gave thanks. It is from the word "thanks" (*eucharisteo*) that the word "Eucharist" is derived. And since he broke the bread after the thanksgiving, the Lord's Supper is also called "the breaking of the bread" (*fractio panis in Latin*).

The words of institution, "This is my body for you" (some manuscripts add the verb "broken" or "given" after "body") have given rise to endless debate. Perhaps the word "body" should be understood in the sense of person. We can be sure that when we eat the bread at the Lord's Table, "he" is present. Fortunately the blessing that comes to us from communion does not depend on our ability to define this presence precisely. C.S. Lewis in *Letters to Malcom* reminds us that Jesus said, "Take eat...," not "Take, understand."

The command of Jesus, "Do this in remembrance of me," should not be understood simply in terms of a mental exercise. The Jewish Passover meal was a re-enactment of the Exodus experience. In a similar way the Eucharist is a kind of reliving of what happened at Calvary. By eating the bread and drinking the cup we are saying "Yes" to the question asked in the Spiritual, "Were you there when they crucified my Lord?"

"In the same manner also the cup," suggests that he took the cup just as he had done with the bread. And since the cup was taken "after the Supper," this may be a reference to the "cup of blessing" mentioned in 10:16. Drinking wine at the Passover meal was obligatory, and usually it was red wine, lending itself better to Jesus' interpretation of it as "the new covenant in my blood" (v. 25).

These words of institution take us back to Sinai where, after Israel had experienced God's deliverance, they entered into covenant with Yahweh — a covenant ratified by blood (Ex. 24:8). Because Israel proved to be a faithless covenant partner, Jeremiah foresaw the day when God would make a "new" covenant (Jer. 31:31-34). That hope was about to be fulfilled when Jesus spoke these words in the upper room. He sealed this new covenant with his blood when he died on Calvary.

"Do this, as often as you drink it, in remembrance of me." He did not say how often the church was to drink it, and churches have come to different conclusions on that point. The early church celebrated Christ's death at the Lord's Table rather frequently, reliving its redemption by eating bread and drinking wine, as our Lord did when he instituted the Supper.

"For as often as you eat this bread and drink this cup you proclaim the Lord's death until he comes" (v. 26). The Eucharist is an acted sermon (the verb is indicative not imperative). The memorial act is a "visible word." Very likely, however, the Eucharist also included a verbal rehearsal of the Passion, just as the Exodus story was rehearsed at the Passover.

"Until he comes" reminds us of Jesus' words about never drinking of the fruit of the vine again until the day when he would drink it "new in the kingdom of God" (Mark 14:25). That this eschatological emphasis was strong in the Eucharistic celebrations of the early church can be seen from the survival of the Aramaic invocation *Marana-tha,* "Our Lord, come" (16:12), as part of the liturgy even in Greek-speaking churches (*Didache* x.6). Marana-tha was probably a prayer invoking the Lord's presence at the Supper something like our "Come, Lord Jesus, be our Guest."

If this is so, then there is a threefold reference in the Lord's Supper: (a) it looks back to the first Easter; (b) it asks for Christ's presence at the table when the church gathers around it; (c) and it calls on the Lord to come in glory (Hunter, *Probing the New Testament,* p. 98). Just as every Lord's day is an anticipation of the Day of the Lord at the end of the age, so every time the church gathers for the Lord's Supper, it has a foretaste of the marriage supper of the Lamb at the end of the age.

### III. Warnings Against the Abuse of the Supper (11:27-34)

Since the bread and cup represented Christ's body and blood, to eat and to drink "in an unworthy manner" was to "be guilty of profaning the body and blood of the Lord" (v. 27). Through lack of love and courtesy, by selfishness and contempt for the poor, the Corinthians violated not only the spirit of brotherhood but they sinned against Christ. The Christian should rather examine himself, lest his behavior should belie his profession. The context suggests that the examination has to do especially with a person's relationship to fellow believers.

Such an examination does not mean that we leave the Lord's Table because of the overwhelming consciousness of our failures and imperfections, but that we seek cleansing by the blood of Christ, and then we can "eat the bread and drink of the cup" (v. 28).

This is a serious matter, for when a believer partakes of Communion without "discerning the body (he) eats and drinks judgment upon himself" (v. 29). Some manuscripts add "of the Lord," after body, to avoid misunderstanding. However, "the body of the Lord" is probably not a reference to Christ's crucified body, but to the church, the body of Christ. By the way they behaved, the Corinthians were not distinguishing the gathering of the church at the Lord's Table from an ordinary meal. Just as it was a violation of the body of Christ when Peter, the Jew, withdrew from table fellowship with the Gentiles, so the Corinthians by their disregard of the poorer fellow Christians, profaned Christ's body.

Paul was of the conviction that abuses at the Lord's Table were the cause of some of the weakness, illness and even death in the Corinthian church (v. 30). (The word "sleep" is a common euphemism for death in the New Testament.) That spiritual faults can have physical consequences was suggested in chapter 5. Such divine judgments might have been averted had the Corinthian believers examined themselves more carefully (v. 31).

But, as in 5:5, where the discipline of the offender is to lead ultimately to his salvation, so God's chastisements are warnings to his children, lest they be condemned together with the unbelieving world (v. 32).

Paul concludes his discussion of the Lord's Supper with a few gentle exhortations. First, when they come together to eat the Lord's Supper they are to be courteous and wait till everyone is there and then eat together, instead of going off by themselves and eating the food they had brought. In this way the poor would not be insulted.

Secondly, if they were so hungry that they could not wait, they should eat at home before they come to the Lord's Table. In that way they could share their food with others in joyous fellowship at church instead of displaying their selfishness and gluttony. Also, it would prevent them from viewing the Lord's Supper as an ordinary meal.

There may have been other details that the Corinthians had asked Paul about, which he could not deal with at the moment. But these can wait until Paul's next visit.

### Personal Response

1. *The Lord's Supper appears to have been practiced in the context of a larger fellowship activity, the love feast (vv.20-23). What is the relationship between the Lord's Supper and fellowship in the church? What are some ways in which believers can practice greater fellowship in the church?*
2. *How can we practice the Lord's Supper so that we remember that the death of Christ was for us personally and for the church corporately?*
3. *Under what circumstances might a person refrain from participating in the Lord's Supper (v. 28)?*

# CHAPTER EIGHTEEN

## Spiritual Gifts

*Now about spiritual gifts, brothers, I do not want you to be
ignorant. You know that when you were pagans, somehow or other
you were influenced and led astray to dumb idols. Therefore I tell
you that no one who is speaking by the Spirit of God says, "Jesus
be cursed," and no one can say, "Jesus is Lord," except by the Holy
Spirit.There are different kinds of gifts, but the same Spirit. There
are different kinds of service, but the same Lord. There are different
kinds of working, but the same God works all of them in all men.*

*Now to each one the manifestation of the Spirit is given for the
common good. To one there is given through the Spirit the message
of wisdom, to another the message of knowledge by means of the
same Spirit, to another faith by the same Spirit, to another gifts of
healing by that one Spirit, to another miraculous powers, to another
prophecy, to another the ability to distinguish between spirits, to
another the ability to speak in different kinds of tongues, and to still
another the interpretation of tongues. All these are the work of one
and the same Spirit, and he gives them to each man, just as he determines (I Corinthians 12:1-11).*

From the opening words of this chapter it could be surmised
that the Corinthians had asked Paul questions about the matter of
spiritual gifts (see I Cor. 7:1). According to the division of this epistle,
Paul devotes three chapters to this subject. In chapter 12 he

introduces the topic; in chapter 13 he lays down a governing principle for the use of gifts, namely love; and in chapter 14 he comes
to grips with the practical issues relating to the use of some of the
gifts in the church. Chapters 12-14, then, represent a triad similar
to the one we discovered in chapters 8-10. Rivalry, envy and pride
were some of the besetting sins of this young Corinthian church.
It led to party-strife in the matter of church leadership, to divisions
among social classes at the Lord's Table and, true to form, there
were quarrels also over spiritual gifts with which the church had
been richly endowed (cf. 1:7).

It appears from Paul's treatment of this subject that those who
had been endowed with gifts that struck the eye prided themselves
on these extraordinary gifts, and those who had received gifts
which were not so obvious in public (as was tongues, for example)
were tempted to be envious.

Spiritual gifts, then, were a third problem area in the public
worship of the Corinthian church (the other two were the head
covering of the woman and disorders at the Lord's Table). Two
words are used to designate these gifts: *pneumatika* (spiritual gifts,
v. 1) and *charismata* (gifts of grace, v. 4). Paul seems to use the two
quite interchangeably, although *peneumatikon* in verse one could be
masculine in gender and refer to "spiritual people."

When Paul says that he does not want his readers to be ignorant about spiritual gifts, he is using a litotes. It's an effective
way of saying that he wants them to be informed.

Whereas the Thessalonians (as appears from I Thess. 5:19,20)
appear to have been wary of some of the gifts bestowed by the
Spirit, the Corinthians evidently made too much of them (at least
of certain gifts). From the relative silence of Paul on this subject in
other letters it should not be inferred that spiritual gifts were not
present in other churches. However, only in Corinth did they
become yet another occasion for strife. But, as has often been
observed facetiously, if Corinth had not had so many problems, we
would not have this marvelous letter!

One question which appears to have been in the mind (and
perhaps in the letter) of the Corinthians was: How does the
presence and the power of the Spirit manifest itself? What is the
telltale sign of an authentic spiritual experience of spiritual
inspiration?

## I. The Test of the Spirit (12:1-3)

Evidently some of the Corinthians held that glossolalia (the gift of tongues) was the surest sign of the presence of the Holy Spirit in their lives. Paul puts the emphasis elsewhere, for ecstasy and glossolalia could be found in pagan worship as well. More important is what a person says and who is the source of his inspiration. To show the difference between paganism and the new life in the Spirit Paul reminds his Gentile readers of their past enslavement to false gods. And while Hellenistic cults were known for ecstatic utterances (the temple of Apollo at Delphi to this day bears witness to the importance of oracular utterances in the ancient world), the pagan gods could not speak, as did Israel's God. It was to such dumb idols that Paul's Gentile readers had formerly been enslaved.

Ecstasy or enthusiasm in worship are not the test of the presence of God's Spirit. Attention must be paid to what is said, particularly, to what is said about Jesus. "No one speaking by the Spirit of God ever says, 'Jesus be cursed'! and no one can say 'Jesus is Lord' except by the Holy Spirit" (v. 3).

We need not infer from this statement that any Corinthian had ever cursed Jesus. When Paul was still an unbeliever he had tried to force Christians to curse Jesus (Acts 26:11). In the persecutions under the Caesars Christians were frequently asked to compromise their faith (with the threat of death) by confessing Caesar as "lord." Unbelieving Jews would curse Jesus (as Paul himself had done before he acknowledged Jesus as Messiah; cf. I Tim. 1:13). There is perhaps some merit in the suggestion that hyperspiritual Corinthians, who felt that only the heavenly Christ was all that mattered, had uttered a curse on the earthly Jesus, who was no longer of any account, as they wrongly thought.

In any case, the Corinthians can be sure that if anyone curses Jesus, he is not inspired to do so by the Holy Spirit. An unmistakable sign of the presence of God's Spirit is the confession of the lordship of Jesus. In fact, only by such a confession could a person hope to be saved (Rom. 10:9,10). "Lord (is) Jesus" (*Kurios Iesous*) is probably the earliest and shortest confession of faith of Gentile Christianity. (Among Jewish Christians it very likely was: "Jesus (is) Messiah" (*Iesous Christos*).

While it is entirely possible for someone to mouth the words "Jesus is Lord," without believing them in his heart, everyone who makes this confession with sincerity does so by the Spirit of God. To acknowledge Christ's lordship in all areas of one's life is a more dependable mark of the presence of the Spirit than ecstasy or even the gift of glossolalia. Jesus said in his Farewell Discourses that the coming Spirit would glorify Jesus (John 16:7). The Spirit must, therefore, not be given a more central place than Jesus Christ.

The real test of authentic Christianity is to be found not so much in the flourishing of striking spiritual gifts, important though these may be, but in lives that are lived humbly under the lordship of Jesus Christ. With that kind of caution, Paul now goes on to describe the great diversity of spiritual gifts.

## II. The Diversity of Gifts (12:4-7)

(a) *The Source of the Gifts* (vv. 4-6). "Now there are varieties of gifts, but the same Spirit; and there are varieties of service, but the same Lord; and there are varieties of working, but it is the same God who inspires them all in everyone."

We should notice the artless trinitarianism of Paul at this point (Spirit, Lord, God). Whereas the word "trinity" is not found in the Bible, the basic elements that were later taken up in the trinitarian formulas are everywhere present in the New Testament. The three persons of the Godhead are not mentioned, however, to explain the diversity of gifts, but point to the unity of the source of all gifts.

The diversity of gifts is due rather to the diversity of needs in the church. To meet these needs the Spirit equips people with different gifts to perform a variety of services in the church. These services are called *diakoniai* (used here not in the technical sense of "deacon" but in the non-technical sense for any kind of service). The Spirit distributes the operations of his power (*energemata*) among God's people to equip them and to inspire them to serve others.

A question that invariably comes up at this point is, how these spiritual gifts relate to our natural endowments. It is as Green suggests, a Gnostic question, for it reflects the notion that what is "natural" is of lesser importance than the "spiritual" (Christ's incarnation would warn against that kind of dichotomy) (*I Believe in the Holy Spirit*, p. 156). F.F. Bruce boldly says that a natural gift when put into the service of God becomes a spiritual gift (*Answers*, p. 207). It is, therefore, quite useless (indeed impossible) to try to establish which gifts we have received supernaturally and which were given to us by heredity, education and practice, now activated by the Holy Spirit. It may even happen that at conversion to Christ, latent gifts are released of which we and others were hardly aware which then become useful in the work of the Kingdom.

(b) *The Purpose of Gifts* (v. 7). "To each is given the manifestation of the Spirit for the common good." It is very important to observe that God does not bestow his gifts *en masse*, but that he puts a great value on the individual. Also, the phrase "to each one" indicates that there is no one in the Body of Christ who has been overlooked in this divine distribution of gifts. Every believer has some gift which enables him or her to serve. The Spirit "manifests" itself by bestowing some gift on each member of the church individually.

However various God's gifts to his children might be, they are given with one purpose in mind: "for the common good" (*sumphoron* means "benefit," "advantage," "profit"). The charisms are not given to us simply as a reward for our spirituality. They are "gifts of grace" (and there was a lot of unspirituality in Corinth where the gifts flourished). Nor are gifts given to us for self-aggrandizement and the inflation of our egos. They have been given to us in order that we might serve others. Others are to profit from our gifts.

We must, therefore, have one concern: Not so much to identify the gifts we have, but rather to serve others. In fact, it is in the process of serving others that we discover where our gifts lie.

### III. Examples of Gifts (12:8-10)

Paul lists nine gifts in the next three verses; others are mentioned at the end of the chapter. Besides, we have lists of gifts in Romans 12 and Ephesians 4. One misreads Paul if it is insisted that whenever a church gathers the nine gifts of our passage should be in evidence.

Various efforts have been made to group these gifts, but perhaps for our purposes we can treat them seriatim.

(a) *The "word of wisdom"* and (b) *the "word of knowledge,"* (v. 8) are two gifts that are hard to distinguish. Both have to do with insight into God's revelation, his ways and his will, which the Spirit gives to some people in greater measure than to others. Added to this gift of insight is that of utterance. It's always a pity when people have profound insights but do not have the ability to express them clearly (although Spurgeon thought people were generally eloquent on those subjects which they understood).

The word of wisdom and knowledge may at times overlap with the prophetic or teaching gift, at other times it may be seen in wise counsel given to the church (or individuals) when the occasion demands it.

(c) *The gift of faith* (v. 9) is not what we call "saving" faith, for all believers have that kind of faith. It is, rather, a special gift of faith, "mountain-moving" faith, as Paul speaks of it in I Corinthians 13:2. It is faith to act in crisis situations, to take risks, to attempt what seems humanly impossible.

One might think of some of the pioneer missionaries, or of those who founded great Christian institutions in the face of overwhelming odds, or people who launched reform and renewal movements in times of spiritual darkness. Perhaps we should list the Christian martyrs among those who had the special gift of faith.

(d) *Gifts of Healings* (v. 9). We do well to notice the plural of both words. There are evidently various kinds of gifts of healing (v. 30). Perhaps Paul also means gifts to heal various kinds of diseases.

The healing ministry of the early church was a kind of afterglow of the healing ministry of Jesus. And that is not to suggest that such healings ceased with the death of the apostles. Healings attended the gospel ministry of Jesus and the apostles. (Healing campaigns, as we hear of them in our day, are foreign to the New Testament.)

Although there were many miraculous cures in the days of the apostles, no one individual possessed the gift to heal all diseases. Evidently Paul had the gift of healing, but was not healed himself (II Cor. 12:8). He admits that he left Trophimus in Miletus because he was sick (II Timothy 4:20) and he counsels Timothy to use wine for medicinal purposes (I Timothy 5:23).

We should rejoice whenever there is evidence of miraculous healing in our day. What we should guard against is the view that the believer can be cured from every illness, if only he will appropriate the benefits of the atonement. Suffering, sickness, disease and death are all part of mankind's lot. Sin needed to be atoned for but not sickness, which came as a consequence of sin. Ultimately, when we enter the gates of glory, both sin and sickness will be banished forever. Here in this life we get but a foretaste of our redemption from sin, and occasionally we get a foretaste of the ultimate redemption of our bodies when God heals in a miraculous way. And the day of miracles is not over, as the next gift so clearly states.

(e) *The Working of Miracles* (v. 10). The doing of mighty works in the age of Jesus and the apostles were signs of the new age. These mighty deeds had enormous evidentiary significance in the early period of the church's mission (and still do). Included in these works of power (*energemata dunameon*) were healings, exorcisms, judgments (smiting Elymas with blindness, for example) and the like.

There is no evidence, however, that a single individual had the power constantly to perform miracles (even though the third century Gregory was given the nickname "Thaumatourgos", i.e. wonder-worker). When Jesus predicted that with the coming of the Spirit his followers would do "greater things" than he had done (John 14:12) he probably had reference to the extent of the church's mission rather than to the magnitude of some single believer's deeds. The God who created this world is free to invade it at any time in ways that boggle the minds of those who are used to the regularity with which this universe functions.

(f) *Prophecy* (v. 10). This was the gift of telling forth the Word of God to meet specific needs, more than the gift of foretelling future events, as can be seen from both Old Testament and New Testament. The predictive element in prophecy is thereby not denied. We see it, for example, in Agabus (Acts 11:28).

A good example of prophecy can be found, for instance, in the seven letters to the churches of Asia. Here Christ through his servant John commends, encourages, criticizes and warns the churches, as each one has need. If we think of prophecy as the declaration of the mind and will of God in the power of the Spirit we shall not be wide of the mark.

Prophets played an important role in the early church. Among them were not only men, but also women (Acts 21:9). When prophets stand together with the apostles as the founders of the church (Eph. 2:20; 3:5), they should perhaps be thought of in the "primary" sense, in contrast to the many prophets who proclaimed God's message in the established churches. (The word "apostle" is also used in the primary sense as well as in the secondary, where it includes all the messengers of the churches.)

(g) *The Ability to Distinguish Between Spirits* (v. 10). Since prophecy was highly valued in the early church, there was a danger of false prophets proclaiming wrong ideas in the name of the Lord. All the members of the churches were, therefore, enjoined to test what was being said by the prophets (I Thess.5:20, 21). In I John 4:1ff, the apostle gives his readers a doctrinal test which they might apply to the teachings they heard. Jesus spoke of the test of character when he observed, "By their fruits you shall know them" (Matthew 7:16).

Paul, however, has in mind a special gift which God gives to some believers to discern between genuine and spurious teaching, authentic and inauthentic Christianity. There is a great need for this gift in our day where we are being served some very mixed and diluted versions of the gospel, especially via the mass media.

The gift of discernment should, however, not be confused with that weakness of the flesh which is manifested by those who suspect every one of being a heretic who does not use precisely their own religious vocabulary. This can hardly be called a gift, but a serious sin, for, according to I Corinthians 13, love is trustful, not suspicious.

(h) *Tongues* and (i) *the interpretation of tongues* (v. 10). There are different "kinds of tongues," says Paul. The speaking in tongues that Paul describes in chapter 14 is obviously different from that on the day of Pentecost. At Pentecost the gift of tongues enabled the apostles to break through all language barriers as they proclaimed the gospel. The gift of tongues in I Corinthians enables the speaker to commune with God in prayer; it is not understood by others. For this reason an added gift was necessary, that is the gift to interpret tongues.

Not all believers had (or have) the gift of tongues (a gift the Corinthians seem to have prized above others and perhaps for that very reason is listed last), and there is no suggestion here or anywhere else in the New Testament that those who had this gift were more spiritual or more useful in the church. But, while there may be much in this area that is spurious, we have no biblical warrant to despise this gift of God's spirit.

Since one and the same Spirit distributes these and other gifts

## IV. The Distribution of Gifts (12:11)

to God's children, we should not be envious of others. Nor should we feel superior to others who may not have our gifts. Moreover, if it is true, as Paul says, that the Spirit bestows gifts "as he wills," we must not dictate to one another which gifts we ought to have or ought to seek after. (There are, of course, "higher gifts" to which we can aspire; cf. 12:31.)

From the present tenses of the verbs in this verse it would not be wrong to infer that the Spirit endows people with gifts for service in accordance with the needs of the church. It should not surprise us, then, if certain gifts recede into the background from time to time and others come to the fore. Certain gifts, of course (such as the gift of teaching), are necessary gifts to carry out that service to which he has called us. And when he asks us to enter a new field of labor, in which we have not yet proved ourselves, we can be confident that he will not ask us to do something for which he does not also equip us. Perhaps one word of warning! When we do our work poorly, let us not be too quick to blame God for withholding the necessary gift. Let us ask, first of all, whether our carelessness and lethargy have not prevented the Spirit from stirring up the gifts that God has given us.

### Personal Response

1. *It is easy to be led astray in a discussion of spiritual gifts (vv. 1-3). What is the central mark of the presence of the Holy Spirit in a believer's life? How is this central mark shown?*
2. *Define "spiritual gifts." List characteristics of people using spiritual gifts. Give examples of how you have seen people use their spiritual gifts.*
3. *There are different kinds of gifts (vv. 4-6). How can we identify which spiritual gift(s) we have? Which gifts do you feel you have?*
4. *How can we "stir up" the spiritual gifts which we have? How can we affirm gifts in other people?*

# CHAPTER NINETEEN

## The Body of Christ

*The body is a unit, though it is made up of many parts; and though all its parts are many, they form one body. So it is with Christ. For we were all baptized by one Spirit into one body — whether Jews or Greeks, slave or free — and we were all given the one Spirit to drink.*

*Now the body is not made up of one part but of many. If the foot should say, "Because I am not a hand, I do not belong to the body," it would not for that reason cease to be part of the body. And if the ear should say, "Because I am not an eye, I do not belong to the body," it would not for that reason cease to be part of the body. If the whole body were an eye, where would the sense of hearing be? If the whole body were an ear, where would the sense of smell be? But in fact God has arranged the parts in the body, every one of them, just as he wanted them to be. If they were all one part, where would the body be? As it is, there are many parts, but one body.*

*The eye cannot say to the hand, "I don't need you"! And the head cannot say to the feet, "I don't need you"! On the contrary, those parts of the body that seem to be weaker are indispensable, and the parts that we think are less honorable we treat with special honor. And the parts that are unpresentable are treated with special modesty, while our presentable parts need no special treatment. But God has combined the members of the body and has given greater honor to the parts that lacked it, so that there should be no division*

141

*in the body, but that its parts should have equal concern for each
other. If one part suffers, every part suffers with it; if one part is
honored, every part rejoices with it.*

*Now you are the body of Christ, and each one of you is a part
of it. And in the church God has appointed first of all apostles, second prophets, third teachers, then workers of miracles, also those
having gifts of healing, those able to help others, those with gifts of
administration, and those speaking in different kinds of tongues.
Are all apostles? Are all prophets? Are all teachers? Do all work
miracles? Do all have gifts of healing? Do all speak in tongues? Do
all interpret? But eagerly desire the greater gifts (I Corinthians
12:12-31).*

In his effort to overcome the tensions that had arisen in the Corinthian church over the gifts of the Spirit, Paul seeks to give his
readers a deeper understanding of the nature of the body of Christ.
Using an analogy from the human body, Paul argues that the body
of Christ is a unity in spite of great diversity among its membership. Moreover, the great variety of gifts which God gives to the different members of the church, should not lead to strife and dissension, but to the healthy functioning of the body of Christ.

To speak of the church as the body of Christ is uniquely
Pauline. What may have suggested this metaphor to the apostle is
not known. Some think Paul derived it from the Hebrew concept
of "corporate personality." Others think he took it over from the
Stoics and transformed it into a Christian concept. Still others sur-
mise that the figure of speech was suggested to Paul by the Last
Supper, where the bread was called Christ's body. But it may also
by simply a Pauline coinage, under the inspiration of God's Spirit.
Paul got an inkling of this concept on the Damascus Road, when
he heard the heavenly Christ say, "Saul, Saul, why do you
persecute me?" To persecute the church, Christ's body, was to
persecute Christ himself.

It is popular today to speak of the church as "the body," and
while this is a biblical metaphor, we should not forget that there are
many other metaphors used in the New Testament to describe the
nature of the church.

In our passage, however, we have the most detailed comparison of the church with the human body found anywhere in the
New Testament. Before he develops this analogy, Paul explains to

his readers how this body of Christ, the church, is constituted.

## I. The Nature of the Body of Christ (12:12,13)

"For just as the body is one and has many members, and all the members of the body, though many, are one body, so it is with Christ" (v. 12).

In Colossians and Ephesians Christ is said to be the "head" of the church, his body. He is the source of the church's life; the church submits in love to his headship; he, the head, supplies its needs.

In Romans 12 and I Corinthians 12 the emphasis lies not on the relation of the body to its head, or vice versa, but rather on the relationship of the members of the body one to another. The cooperation of the individual members, diverse as they may be, contributes to the well-being of the total community.

The question now is: How did this body of Christ come into being? Paul's answer is that the Corinthians "were all baptized into one body by one Spirit — Jews or Greeks, slaves or free — and all were made to drink of one Spirit" (v. 13).

There are six other passages in the Gospels and Acts which speak of the baptizing work of the Spirit. In each of the four Gospels John the Baptist promises that the greater One will baptize with the Holy Spirit (Mt. 3:11; Mk.1:8; Lk. 3:16; Jn. 1:33). Jesus explains that promise as a reference to Pentecost (Acts 1:5), and when the spirit fell on the household of Cornelius, Peter was reminded of the fulfillment of John's prediction of the coming Spirit baptism at Pentecost (Acts 11:16).

In all these six passages the baptism of the Spirit is a reference to Pentecost, when the church was founded through the outpouring of the Holy Spirit. I Corinthians 12:13 is the only other passage in the New Testament in which the baptizing work of the Spirit is referred to and again it speaks of the founding of the church and the initiation of those who believed into the body of Christ.

What should be observed is that "all" the Corinthians were baptized by the Spirit into Christ's body. Not all believers are "filled" with the Spirit, but all are baptized by the Spirit. Without the baptism of the Spirit they could not be members of the church.

This baptism into the body of Christ by the Holy Spirit was then demonstrated publicly by baptism with water. In this early period conversion, the gift of the Spirit and baptism with water were all part of the beginning of the Christian life. And to be baptized with water implied membership in a local church.

It's a pity that some pastors separate baptism from church membership. Such a view betrays a misunderstanding of the church as the body of Christ. The body of Christ into which the Spirit baptizes us at conversion is not some invisible, nebulous body, but is to be found in Corinth, Ephesus and Philippi. To be baptized by the Spirit into Christ's body implies, therefore, baptism with water into the body of Christ in a given locality. That this is so can be seen from Paul's reference to Jew and Greek, slave and free. All these radical and social differences had been overcome by baptism through the Spirit into the one body of Christ at Corinth.

The expression, "and all were made to drink of one Spirit," is just another way of describing the receipt of the Spirit at conversion. The language is reminiscent of John 7:37-39, where John explains Jesus' invitation to the thirsty to come and drink as a reference to the Holy Spirit which those who believed in Jesus were to receive. It speaks of the refreshment and life which the Spirit brings to those who put their thrust in Christ.

## II. Harmony in the Body of Christ (12:14-26)

Paul will now argue that diversity in the body of Christ, as in the human body, does not destroy its unity. A body consisting of one organ only would be a kind of monstrosity (v. 14). Diversity in the human body is not a problem, but is essential for its existence.

How ridiculous to think that the foot should say, "Because I am not a hand, I do not belong to the body" (v. 16). This illustration reflects the temptation of the less-endowed members in the Corinthian church to be envious of those who had more outstanding gifts. Similarly, if the ear should say, "Because I am not an eye, I do not belong to the body," it would be no less a member of the body (v. 16).

How grotesque to think of the whole body as an eye or an ear (v. 17)! Then why should the members of Christ's body want to be alike? In God's infinite wisdom he arranged the organs of the body as he chose (v. 18). How monstrous if our entire bodies were one organ (v. 19)! Thankfully, while there are many parts to our body, there is one unified organism (v. 20).

And so one organ of the body, such as the eye, cannot say to another, such as the hand, "I have no need of you" (v. 21). Similarly, those members of Christ's body who have outstanding gifts cannot do without those who have gifts that do not strike the eye. No member of the body of Christ is independent of the other.

Often those parts of the body which seem weaker are most indispensable (v. 22). One might think of vital organs such as heart, lungs, liver and kidneys, without which life could not go on (v. 22). It would be precarious, therefore, to pass judgment too cavalierly on the relative significance of someone's gifts.

It is not quite clear what Paul has in mind with the "less presentable" organs which are given special honor in that they are covered. Does he mean that the internal organs are covered by flesh, or does he mean, for example, the genitalia, which are covered with clothes (v. 23)? Those organs fit for public display (such as the eye) we do not cover; they do not need the adornment of clothes (v. 24a).

In his sovereignty God has adjusted the functions and relations of the members of the body in such a way that there is no discord in the body (v. 24b). So interdependent are the various members that they exercise the same care for one another. And because all the members are inter-related, "if one member suffers, all suffer together." When we hurt our finger we do not simply say, "My finger hurts," but " I have pain in my finger" — our whole body is drawn into the suffering of one member. And we all know how pain in one little tooth can cause the entire body to suffer. There is discord in the body when one of its members fails to function.

On the other hand, "if one member is honored, all rejoice together" (v. 26). There is no pride or jealousy among the members of the human body. If only this could always be said of the members of the church! It was certainly not the case in Corinth.

### III. Gifts to the Body of Christ (12:27-31)

This rather drawn-out analogy between the human body and the body of Christ is now brought to bear on the use of the spiritual gifts in the church. Wherever a church is found, there is the body of Christ, and the men and women who belong to it are the members of this body. Each member, as Paul has illustrated, has a God-given function to perform, and to fulfill this function God has given individual members different gifts.

Eight kinds of members with special functions are listed. There are both similarities and differences between this list of gifts and the nine mentioned in verses 8-10. To say that God has "appointed" certain members to fulfill a special function in the church is to underscore the sovereignty of God in the distribution of his gifts.

The apostle's, prophets and teachers are set off from the rest since they had such an important function in the founding of the church. In Ephesians 4:11 "evangelists" are added to apostles, prophets and teachers. In Ephesians 2:20 the apostles and prophets are singled out as constituting the foundation of the church.

Apostles, in the primary sense of that word, were witnesses to the Christ-event. They were not replaced when they died (as were bishops or elders). As those who had seen the risen Christ, they founded the church; others built on this foundation.

Prophets declared God's will to the people of God in the power of the Spirit. They, like the teachers, were not necessarily apostles, but the apostles were prophets and teachers. The same person might also be a prophet and a teacher (Acts 13:1). In all the lists of charisms the preaching gift is paramount, for the church cannot mature unless converts are instructed in the basic tenets of the Christian faith.

But God has given the church other gifted members as well. There are the workers of miracles (see v. 10) and "the gifts of healings" (notice again the plural as in verse 9). A gift not mentioned in the earlier list is that of "helpers" (or "helps"). Perhaps the gift of helps is a reference to the diaconic ministries in the church, the care of the poor and the needy.

Some of these gifts appear to be so natural in character that we find it hard to see them as charisms. But, as we have said earlier, Paul makes no effort to distinguish between the natural and the supernatural. It comes as a surprise to some readers to see the gift of "administration" listed with such charisms as healings and tongues. The word Paul uses is a nautical term, taken from the world of shipping. *Kubernesis* comes from *kubernetes* (the helmsman of a ship) and has given us the modern word "cybernetics." The gift of leadership is just as much a spiritual gift as is the gift to do miracles, and is a very necessary gift for the life of the church. Once again Paul concludes his list of *charismata* with the gift of tongues and then asks a series of rhetorical questions to which the implied answer is No! "Are they all apostles?" No! "Are they all prophets?" No! "Are all teachers?"

No! "Do all work miracles?" No! "Do all possess gifts of healing?" No! "Do all speak in tongues?" No! "Do all interpret?" No!

These seven questions represent a third list of spiritual gifts and again tongues is put at the bottom. One cannot help but infer from this that Paul is deliberately minimizing the importance of this gift over others. Also, this series of questions should lay to rest the false notion that the sign of the fulness of the Spirit (or the "baptism" — when understood in a different sense from the one in the New Testament) is the gift of tongues. The entire argument has been that the body of Christ is characterized by diversity, but this diversity (as seen in the different gifts) does not destroy the unity of the body of Christ.

As if to prepare us for the discussion of the "higher gifts" in chapter 14, Paul concludes this paragraph with the exhortation to be zealous for the "greater" gifts. Among the greater gifts is that of prophecy as will become obvious from chapter 14.

Just how this desire for the greater gifts is to express itself Paul does not say. He does mention that where people have the gift of tongues without the gift of interpretation they might pray for this added gift (14:13). To pray for a necessary gift is, then, a legitimate way of expressing the desire for greater gifts. Certainly it would also include openness on the part of the believer to receive whatever gift God wanted to give him. Gifts must not be desired, however, for purpose of display, but always with the intention of serving others and to build up the church.

Whether Paul means that love should govern our desire for greater gifts or whether love is the way *par excellence*, regardless of any gifts, is not quite clear. From chapter 13 it appears as if love is much more important than any *charismata;* indeed, the spiritual gifts are of no avail where love is lacking. To put it differently, the "fruit of the Spirit" (love, joy, peace, etc.) is much more important than the "gifts" of the Spirit. But more of that in the next chapter.

### Personal Response

1. *Paul likens the church to a human body (vv. 12-13). List ways the church is like a body.*
2. *Think of your local congregation. How is it functioning like a body?*
3. *We tend to say that some functions in the church are more important than others. This we should not do (vv. 14-26). List as many functions in the church as you can think of. What would happen if any one of*

*them were missing?*
4. *How can we recognize the importance of all the gifts in the church?*

# CHAPTER TWENTY

## The Greatest of These is Love

*And now I will show you the most excellent way. If I speak in the tongues of men and of angels, but have not love, I am only a resounding gong or a clanging cymbal. If I have the gift of prophecy and can fathom all mysteries and all knowledge, and if I have a faith that can move mountains, but have not love, I am nothing. If I give all I possess to the poor and surrender my body to the flames, but have not love, I gain nothing.*

*Love is patient, love is kind. It does not envy, it does not boast, it is not proud. It is not rude, it is not self-seeking, it is not easily angered, it keeps no record of wrongs. Love does not delight in evil but rejoices with the truth. It always protects, always trusts, always hopes, always perseveres.*

*Love never fails. But where there are prophecies, they will be stilled; where there is knowledge, it will pass away. For we know in part and we prophesy in part, but when perfection comes, the imperfect disappears. When I was a child, I talked like a child, I thought like a child, I reasoned like a child. When I became a man, I put childish ways behind me. Now we see but a poor reflection; then we shall see face to face. Now I know in part; then I shall know fully, even as I am fully known.*

*And now these three remain; faith, hope and love. But the greatest of these is love (I Corinthians 13:1-13).*

From a literary point of view I Corinthians 13 is a high water-mark in the Pauline correspondence. At times one doesn't know whether it's prose or poetry. Perhaps one could call it a didactic poem or hymn in praise of the supreme quality of the Christian life, namely "love."

The Greek language with all its richness, incapable of express-ing this new concept of love with its more common words, such as *philia* and *eros*, under the guidance of the Spirit, invested a rather more obscure word, *agape*, with new connotations and depths.

One always has some hesitations about examining Paul's song on the supremacy of love. One feels a bit like the person examining a rose, plucking petal after petal, only to find in the end that the rose has been destroyed. Moreover, no one can honestly go through a chapter like this without feeling torn between the ideal that is here presented and one's failures to live up to this ideal.

The chapter can be discussed in a meaningful way quite in-dependent of its context. It should not be forgotten, however, that chapter 13 is the center-piece of a trilogy of chapters on spiritual gifts. Paul will argue in this chapter that without love to regulate the use of the *charismata* all the gifts of the Spirit are of no significance.

## I. The Importance of Love (13:1-3)

Whereas the gift of tongues came at the end of the line in the three lists given in chapter 12, it stands at the top now that Paul is about to show the relative insignificance of gifts when compared with love. Paul declares that if he had "the tongues of men and angels," but had not love, he would be but a noisy gong or clanging cymbal (v. 1). Does he mean ordinary and supernatural, or earthly and heavenly tongues? In Jewish tradition there is reference to a few choice souls who could speak in angels' tongues. Presumably these had a greater range and more beauty than human tongues. Generally it was held that the angels spoke Hebrew.

It is unlikely that Paul had much interest in the question of what language angels spoke. What he wanted to say was that even if he possessed the whole gamut of tongues, without love all would be reduced to the level of paganism. That seems to be suggested by the musical instruments, the echoing bronze and the *kumbalon* (our "cymbal") *alalazon* (an onomatopoeic word recalling the constant beat and the shrill tone of the cymbal in pagan worship).

Love is also greater than prophecy (one of the "greater" gifts according to chapter 14). In order to prophesy one has to be able to look into God's "mysteries," that is, God's revelation which was hidden in the ages before the coming of Christ. But even the ability to comprehend divine revelation and to penetrate the depths of the knowledge of God is nothing compared to love.

Similarly the gift of "faith" (cf. 12:9), by which a person can move mountains, is of no significance without love (v. 2). "To move mountains" is a figure of speech for doing the impossible. Jesus also used this metaphor (Matthew 17:20f). The mountain stands for insurmountable obstacles, and some people are given the strength to accomplish the impossible. But such a gift also fades into nothing when compared with love (v. 2).

Conceivably a person could even convert all his property into morsels of food for the poor without genuine love. This was obviously not the case when Barnabas gave all that he possessed to the poor (Acts 4:36). In the case of Ananais and Sapphira, however, motives other than love were in effect.

Even a martyr's death without love brings no gain. "If I deliver my body to be burned" reminds one of the three Hebrews and others like them who went into the fire for their faith (Daniel 3:28). The supreme sacrifice of life, however, if it springs from other motives than love, is valueless in the sight of God and profits nothing (v. 3).

The latest edition of the Greek New Testament of the United Bible Societies reads: "If I should deliver my body in order that I may boast" (*kauchesomai*). The difference between "burned" (*kauthesomai*) and "boast" (*kauchesomai*) is one letter. The manuscript evidence favors "boast." Quite obviously if one sacrifices oneself for other reasons than love, one gains nothing.

## II. The Character of Love (13:4-7)

In the second stanza of this magnificent hymn on Christian love Paul sings about the basic characteristics of *agape* and tells us what love does and does not do. "Love is patient and kind." These two expressions of love are particularly conspicuous in God's dealings with mankind (e.g. Romans 2:4). Long-suffering and kindness are also a fruit of the Spirit (Galatians 4:22). They speak not of a limp acquiescence, but of a patient perseverance in the face of injury received.

To lay bare the true nature of *agape* Paul mentions a number of things love does not do. "Love is not jealous." The verb *zeloo* means to be zealous, but when used in the negative sense, as here (compare the positive meaning in 12:31), it means to be jealous and envious.

Love does not play the braggart. The verb *pepereuetai* occurs only here in the New Testament and denotes empty boasting. It is not too different from arrogance. To be "puffed up" (*phusioo*) was a constant temptation for some Corinthians (cf.4:6,18,19; 5:2; 8:1).

Love is not rude. In 7:36 this verb (*aschemoneo*) is rendered as "not behaving properly." It suggests unseemly or unmannerly conduct, such as manifested itself in Corinth at the Lord's Table.

Love does not seek its own interests or insist on its own way. In such matters as party-strife, the insistence on one's rights, eating by oneself, instead of sharing one's food, flourishing one's gifts in the meetings of the church, the readers revealed that kind of selfishness that tends to afflict us all. It was from the slavery of our egos that Christ came to set us free.

Love is not provoked to anger. The word *paroxusmos* (here the verb) is used in the positive sense when we are exhorted to "provoke one another to love and good works" (Hebrews 10:24), but here it means "irritability." Love does not take offence quickly; it is not resentful. More inveterate anger expresses itself in keeping a record of wrongs; something love does not do. To keep record means to be unforgiving, to look for revenge. Henry Ward Beecher once said that everyone should have a fair-sized cemetery in which to bury the faults of his friends.

Love "does not rejoice at wrong, but rejoices in the right" (v. 6). There is a stern, moral quality in love; it cannot call black, white. It hates injustice, corruption and cruelty. Love does not "gloat over other men's sins" (NEB). However, to rejoice at wrong may also have the connotation of what is known in German as *Schadenfreude* — to rejoice at the loss, the plight, the downfall of someone we do not particularly like.

After a series of negatives Paul turns to positives. He mentions four things love does:

(i) "Love bears all things" (v. 7). The verb "to bear" (*stego*) can mean to cover or to hide, and it's quite possible that this is the meaning here, in keeping with I Peter 4:8, where we are told that "love covers a multitude of sins." Moffatt gives it as: "Love...is slow to expose." Alfred Kuen renders it in French as: " L'amour couvre tout" (love covers everything). There are occasions where we need to pass over in silence what we know of others, when to make it public would lead to much harm.

(ii) "Love...believes all things." Surely Paul does not mean that love is gullible. He himself did not believe all he heard about the Corinthians (11:18). But love is always eager to believe the best. Perhaps "believe" is used in the sense of "trust." The French commentator Hering gives it as *plein de foi* (full of trust). Love is not suspicious. Love keeps faith in others, even when they fail.

(iii) "Love...hopes all things." It is ready to give an offender a second chance. When it hears an evil rumor it hopes it won't be true or, at least, it won't be quite so bad. Love forgives "seventy times seventy" (Matthew 18:22). Perhaps no one illustrates this characteristic of love as do parents who are in pain because a child has gone wrong but who never give up the hope that God's grace will yet reclaim their son or daughter.

Finally, (iv) "Love endures all things." Not stoic resignation but joyful acceptance of suffering and hardship for the sake of Christ and his kingdom is meant. Love remains steadfast under the burdens God asks us to bear — to endure wrongs, losses, disappointments. "Love is not love that alters when it alteration finds" (Shakespeare).

## III. The Permanence of Love (13:8-13)

Love is greater than spiritual gifts, since it remains forever, whereas the gifts are for this life only. "Love never ends" (v. 8). It never "falls down," as the text reads literally. By contrast, the gift of prophecy "shall be put out of commission," tongues "shall cease of themselves," the gift of knowledge "shall be made inoperative" (not knowledge as such, but that special kind of knowledge of God's will that believers need for this life and which is always more or less inadequate).

In contrast to the fulness of revelation that lies in store for those who love God (cf. 2:9), our knowledge here on earth is imperfect. And because we know "in part," we can prophesy only "in part"

(v. 9). But when the perfect comes, the imperfect shall pass away"
(v. 10). Four times in close succession the verb *katargeo* (literally
"to put completely out of work") occurs — translated by KJV as
"fail," "vanish away," "be done away," "put away," respectively.

The three gifts (prophecy, tongues, faith) are illustrative of
what happens to all the *charismata* when this age comes to an end
and we enter the gates of eternity. They are given to the church for
its own upbuilding, for in this age the church is never perfect, but
when the church is taken to glory it enters perfection and has no
need of the gifts of the Spirit any longer. The "perfect" (*teleion*) is
not a reference to the post-apostolic church, which was no more
perfect than the apostolic. Nor does it refer to the completion of the
New Testament Canon, as some have argued. Such explanations
arise out of the desire to limit some of the spiritual gifts, mentioned
in the New Testament, to the apostolic period. But the church
needs these gifts as long as it is in the state of imperfection. Only
the Parousia makes the gifts redundant.

To illustrate this, Paul compares the church to the passage of
a child to full manhood. "When I was a child, I spoke like a child,
I thought like a child, I reasoned like a child; when I became a man,
I gave up childish ways" (v. 11). Paul does not mean that speaking
in tongues is a sign of babyhood, but rather that the present state
of our existence is to our future perfection as childhood is to
maturity. No doubt there is an oblique warning in this illustration
not to get too excited about the gifts of the Spirit, for they belong
to the age of the church's immaturity.

Another illustration is the mirror, which does not allow us to
see reality directly, but indirectly. Corinthian polished metal mir-
rors were famous, but even they offered the viewer but an imperfect vision of himself. So it is with our understanding and com-
prehension of God's ways in this life. "We see in a mirror dimly."
Literally translated, the text reads, "We see by means of a mirror
into a riddle." Our vision is often distorted, we are puzzled, we
have to say "perhaps" again and again.

"But when the Lord comes we shall see "face to face" (v. 12).
The word play *prosopon pros prosopon* (face facing face) is lost in the
translation. In eternity our vision will be direct and clear. Leaving
the figure of speech behind, Paul declares that his partial and imperfect knowledge (*ginosko* — to know) shall give way to perfect

knowledge (*epiginosko* — to know fully is that *Visio Dei* for which the saints have longed throughout the ages).

The gifts of the Spirit, good and necessary as they are, partake of the imperfections of this age and pass away when this age ends. By contrast, "faith hope, and love abide, these three, but the greatest of these is love" (v. 13). This triad, faith, hope and love, appears again and again in Paul's letters, as in the writings of other apostles. Faith, hope and love are of the very essence of the Christian life and, therefore, are not ephemeral, as are the gifts of the Spirit. When one recalls that to hope in God or to believe in him are different ways of describing a relationship of trust, we easily see that this relationship continues throughout eternity.

But whatever the form of faith and hope in the beyond, love is the greatest of the three. In verse 7 it was said that love "believes all things," "hopes all things." Love remains unchanged in its nature even when we enter the gates of perfection.

Not all believers have the same gift but "the love of God has been poured into the hearts of all the saints by the Holy Spirit which has been given to us" (Romans 5:5).

### Personal Response

1. *Chapter thirteen is in the context of a discussion of spiritual gifts in chapters twelve and fourteen. What is the relationship between love and the exercise of spiritual gifts?*
2. *Verses four through seven give several positive and negative characteristics of love. How do you rate on each characteristic? How does your church rate?*
3. *Christians grow from childhood to adult maturity (vv. 9-12). Trace the progress in your life from putting away childish things to putting on adult maturity. What kind of things did you put away and what kind of things did you put on?*
4. *Share examples of times when love ruled your life.*
5. *What is the relationship between love and evangelism/service?*

# CHAPTER TWENTY-ONE

## Tongues and Prophecy

*Follow the way of love and eagerly desire spiritual gifts, especially the gift of prophecy. For anyone who speaks in a tongue does not speak to men but to God. Indeed, no one understands him; he utters mysteries with his spirit. But everyone who prophesies speaks to men for their strengthening, encouragement and comfort. He who speaks in a tongue edifies himself, but he who prophesies edifies the church. I would like everyone of you to speak in tongues, but I would rather have you prophesy. He who prophesies is greater than one who speaks in tongues, unless he interprets, so that the church may be edified.*

*Now, brothers, if I come to you and speak in tongues, what good will I be to you, unless I bring you some revelation or knowledge or prophecy or word of instruction? Even in the case of lifeless things that make sounds, such as the flute or harp, how will anyone know what tune is being played unless there is a distinction in the notes? Again, if the trumpet does not sound a clear call, who will get ready for battle? So it is with you. Unless you speak intelligible words with your tongue, how will anyone know what you are saying? You will just be speaking into the air. Undoubtedly there are all sorts of languages in the world, yet none of them is without meaning. If then I do not grasp the meaning of what someone is saying, I am a foreigner to the speaker, and he is a foreigner to me. So it is with you. Since you are eager to have spiritual gifts, try to excel in gifts that build up the church.*

*For this reason the man who speaks in a tongue should pray that he may interpret what he says. For if I pray in a tongue, my spirit prays, but my mind is unfruitful. So what shall I do? I will pray with my spirit, but I will also pray with my mind; I will sing with my spirit, but I will also sing with my mind. If you are praising God with your spirit, how can one who finds himself among those who do not understand say "Amen" to your thanksgiving, since he does not know what you are saying? You may be giving thanks well enough, but the other man is not edified.*

*I thank God that I speak in tongues more than all of you. But in the church I would rather speak five intelligible words to instruct others than ten thousand words in a tongue.*

*Brothers, stop thinking like children. In regard to evil be infants, but in your thinking be adults. In the Law it is written: "Through men of strange tongues and through the lips of foreigners I will speak to this people, but even then they will not listen to me," says the Lord.*

*Tongues, then, are a sign, not for believers but for unbelievers; prophecy, however, is for believers, not for unbelievers. So if the whole church comes together and everyone speaks in tongues, and some who do not understand or some unbelievers come in, will they not say that you are out of your mind? But if any unbeliever or someone who does not understand comes in while everybody is prophesying, he will be convinced by all that he is a sinner and will be judged by all, and the secrets of his heart will be laid bare. So he will fall down and worship God, exclaiming, "God is really among you!" (I Corinthians 14:1-25).*

This chapter is closely linked to the great hymn on Christian *agape* (chap. 13) by its opening exhortation, "Make love your aim." Paul uses a strong and vivid figure of speech in the first word of the chapter. "Go after," "pursue" *agape*, is his command. (*Dioko* — to chase — is a characteristic Pauline metaphor for spiritual endeavor.) This is the "more excellent way" of which Paul spoke in 13:31b.

The second part of 14:1 latches on to 13:31a, "But earnestly desire the higher gifts." Among these "higher" or "greater" gifts prophecy stands out. Paul now devotes a major portion of chapter 14 to a comparison of tongues and prophecy. Some Corinthians, carried away by the mystery and the ecstasy associated with tongues, gave to this gift a significance in relation to other charismata quite out of keeping with the purpose of the gifts. While recognizing the place of tongues in private devotion, Paul argues that in the public worship of the church those gifts which lead to the upbuilding of the believers should receive preference. Let us follow him in his argument.

## I. Prophecy Superior to Tongues for the Believer (14:2-19)

(a) *The Argument* (vv. 2-6). One reason prophecy (the gift of proclaiming God's will and speaking to the needs of the church) is superior to tongues is that it is given in words people can understand. Tongues, by contrast, cannot be understood, for the speaker "utters mysteries in the Spirit" (v. 2). Whereas the gift of tongues at Pentecost enabled the apostles to speak so that all the visitors could hear the message in their mother tongues, here the speaking in tongues is not understood by others. It may be a very meaningful experience for those who have this gift to speak to God "in a tongue," but for the church it is more important that one speak "to men" if others are to benefit.

If one speaks to people in a language they can understand, as does the Christian prophet (v. 3), they can be "built up." This architectural metaphor (*oikodome* — to build up) occurs repeatedly in this passage. It speaks of the kind of instruction and exhortation that leads to the deepening, enriching and strengthening of the faith of the believers. The three words standing next to "upbuilding" could be viewed as expressions or interpretations of "upbuilding."

Prophetic teaching encourages the congregation. The word *paraklesis* means, among other things, comfort, strength, help, encouragement, and so the English versions vary a whole lot in the way they render it. Every congregation has need of encouragement — they not only long for it; they really need it. People listen for a word on Sunday morning that will put heart into them for the week.

Closely related to "encouragement" is the word "consolation" (*paramuthia* — to console by speaking). Joseph Parker of London advised preachers always to speak to wounded hearts, for every congregation had them. "Never morning wears to evening but some heart does break." But encouragement and consolation can come to people only if they understand what is being said. "He who speaks in tongues edifies himself, but he who prophecies, edifies the church" (v. 4). It would, therefore be a serious failure in love and a crass example of selfishness if someone with the gift of tongues insisted on using that gift in a public meeting of the church.

But, lest the Corinthians should infer that Paul despises the gift of tongues, he expresses the wish that they might all speak in tongues, although he knows that God gives that gift to whom he wills. However, he would rather than they had the gift of prophecy. "He who prophecies is greater than he who speaks in tongues, unless someone interprets, so that the church be edified" (v. 5).

Paul recognizes tongues as a legitimate gift from God and if people could understand what was being said in tongues they could indeed be edified. But since they can't understand, there is need for interpretation. Whether this interpretation was to be done by the speaker himself or by another member of the church is not stated. What is important for us to observe is that only what is understood can edify. Preachers, therefore, must learn to express themselves clearly, and listeners must come to church prepared to think, if they are to be built up. If Paul should come to Corinth and speak in tongues, as we say, he would be of little benefit to the congregation, unless he brought "some revelation or knowledge or prophecy or teaching" (v. 6). Perhaps one could say that revelation and knowledge have to do with insight into God's salvatory plans, his will and his ways, while prophecy and teaching represent the gifts for the communication of these insights. The important point is that if Paul should speak God's message to the church in the Greek language, which they spoke, they would be built up. This would not be the case if he spoke in tongues.

(b) *The Illustrations* (vv. 7-13). In support of his argument that tongues are inferior to prophecy, Paul takes an illustration from the realm of musical instruments (vv. 7-9). He calls them "lifeless," for they are made of wood, metal or what have you. The flute (a wind instrument) and the harp (a stringed instrument) are dead, inanimate objects until someone who can play them brings them to life by making a meaningful variation of notes. Without such a distinction of tones people will not know what is being played (v. 7).

Or to use another illustration, there is the bugle. If it gives an indistinct sound, who will get ready for battle (v. 8)? If a sound is to serve as a signal it must be clear. Soldiers do not know whether to advance or retreat if the signal is not clear.

The application to speaking in tongues is obvious. If someone says something in a tongue that is not intelligible (*eusemos* means "easy to understand"; *semaino* gives us the word "semantics"), then how shall anyone know what is being said? A speaker who discourses in an unknown tongue will speak into the air; and nothing robs a speaker more quickly of the desire to speak than the realization that he is speaking into the air.

Following the illustration from musical instruments, Paul takes an illustration from the realm of human languages — an illustration even more closely related to tongues than the one from musical instruments. There are many kinds of languages in the world (*phonai* can mean voices, noises, sounds, languages) and none without meaning (v. 10). (Our professor of Linguistics at the University of British Columbia claimed he could give 14 different meanings to the Chinese "i" sound, depending on the modulation of the voice.) "But if I do not know the meaning of the language, I shall be a foreigner to the speaker and the speaker a foreigner to me" (v. 11). The Greek word for foreigner is *barbaros* ("barbarian" — an onomatopoeic word, the root meaning of which is "stuttering," "stammering," "uttering unintelligible sounds"), and those who have travelled in foreign countries know how difficult it is to communicate when one doesn't know the language of the country.

Again the application to tongues is obvious. If someone in church speaks with tongues the hearers will not understand and the speaker will be to them like a "barbarian," uttering gibberish.

Since then the Corinthians are "zealots for spiritual things," that is, eager for the manifestations of the Spirit, they should strive rather to excell in building up the church (v. 12). This they would do if they exercised the gift of prophecy rather than the gift of tongues. If tongues are to be exercised at all in public then they must be interpreted, so that people can understand what is being said. And if a believer who speaks in tongues does not have this gift of interpretation, he might pray for it. This would presumably be one way of "desiring" a gift (12:31). Again we see that gifts are bestowed by God not to puff up the recipient, but to enable him to serve others.

(c) *The Practice* (vv. 14-19). Using himself as example, Paul explains that when he prays in tongues, his spirit prays, but his mind is unfruitful (v. 14). Whether the word "spirit" (*pneuma*) is to be understood as Holy Spirit or whether it is simply the inner man is not quite clear. "Spirit" is distinguished from "mind" in our text.

Paul had the gift of speaking in tongues and when he engaged in prayer he felt inwardly lifted up, but his prayer was not intelligent to others. It is not likely that the apostle here has the praying "with sighs too deep for words" in mind (Rom. 8:26), since that is the experience of all believers.

However, Paul will pray not only "with the spirit" but also "with the mind" (v. 15). Praying intelligently, so that others can understand his prayer, is the kind of praying Paul will engage in in public. Also, he will sing "with the mind" in public, for then others can understand and even join in. But he will also sing in the spirit. Presumably he will do this in his private devotions since others would not understand this kind of singing.

With a touch of irony Paul suggests that if a Corinthian blesses God "with the spirit," that is, if he speaks a prayer of thanksgiving in tongues, the "outsider" will not be able to say "Amen" to the thanksgiving since he cannot understand what is being said. The practice of the congregation to join in the Amen at the end of doxologies and prayers was carried over into the Christian church from the Jewish synagogue. Those who said "Amen" properly were promised a rich reward by God said some of the rabbis. It's a pity that some churches are losing the practice of responding with a hearty "Amen" to public prayers.

Just who is meant by the "outsider" is not clear. In verse 24 he is distinguished from the unbeliever. The Greek word *idiotes* is derived from *idios,* meaning a private, uninitiated, lay person. Perhaps Paul has the young, inexperienced Christian in mind, or the one who doesn't have the gift of tongues, who would feel "put down" and left out when those with the gift spoke in tongues.

What goes on in church is to be intelligible. What is said in tongues is perfectly intelligible to God and so Paul can say — again with a tinge of irony — "you give thanks beautifully, but the other person is not built up" (v. 17). What is not understood can't build up. Therefore, to speak in tongues which can't be understood by others is a violation of the law of love. And, as Paul pointed out in chapter 13, love is more important than any or all of the spiritual gifts.

Perhaps some of Paul's readers may have thought that such a denigration of tongues could come only from a person who did not have this gift, and so quickly adds, "I thank God that I speak in tongues more than all of you" (v. 18). With that the charge of "sour grapes" falls to the ground. Also, Paul's gratefulness to God for the gift of tongues should silence the critics who may have felt Paul was slighting this gift. It's a master-touch! Who would have thought that Paul spoke in tongues had he not told us so?

Although he is thankful for the gift of tongues, in church he "would rather speak five words with (his) mind, in order to instruct others, than ten thousand words in a tongue" (v. 19). A few meaningful words, intelligible to the audience, are much more effective than "myriads" (Greek: *myrios*) of unintelligible words, for by intelligible word the church is instructed. To be instructed (*katecho* — catechize) evidently is a rough equivalent for being built up.

The gist of Paul's argument up to this point has been that prophecy is of more significance for the believer in Christian worship than tongues because it is understood and therefore edifies the church. He will now show that the same argument holds for unbelievers who may choose to attend a Christian worship service.

## II. Prophecy Superior to Tongues for Unbelievers (14:20-25)

Before Paul begins the next round in his argumentation, he calls on his readers affectionately ("brothers") not to be children in their thinking (v. 20). A preference for tongues over against intelligent speech was a sign not of higher spirituality but of immaturity. One area in which child-like innocence is commendable is that of evil. Paul is not encouraging ignorance of the evil in and around us, but he would rather his readers were (or remained) inexperienced in evil.

Paul begins by quoting a passage from Isaiah 28:11, 12 (by the "law", in which this passage is written, he means the OT). The prophet Isaiah warned his contemporaries that if they refused to listen to God's message, communicated in the Hebrew tongue, which they understood, then he would speak to them by men of strange tongues and by the lips of foreigners. But the prophet's hearers mocked him for using baby-talk (Isaiah 28:10), and so brought upon themselves the Assyrians whose language they did not understand. This unfamiliar language was for Judah, then, a sign of divine judgement.

This unfamiliar language was for Judah, then, a sign of divine judgment.

If, therefore, unbelievers should enter the Corinthian congregation and they should hear the members all speaking in tongues, they would become contemptuous and confirmed in their unbelief by tongues. Tongues then are not a saving sign but a sign of condemnation for the unbeliever (as foreign tongues were for ancient unbelieving Israel). Prophecy by contrast, creates believers, bringing them to faith.

Young Christians, or those not versed in tongues, together with unbelievers would think the Corinthians had gone mad if they should hear them speak in tongues in public. Quite the opposite would be the effect of prophecy on the unbeliever. He would be convicted by the word spoken by Christian prophets and called to account for his deeds. The word would pierce directly to his heart, it would expose his inmost being, it would convict him of sin. Assuming that the unbeliever opens his heart to the voice of God, he will fall on his face, worship God, and declare that God is really among them. No question, then, that the proclamation of God's words in an intelligible way is of much greater value for both the church in worship as well as for the unbeliever who should happen to attend.

There is no suggestion, here, that the Christian prophets preached at the visiting unbelievers. They spoke for the edification of the church and the unbelievers heard the good news of the gospel and embraced the Christian faith. Christians who befriend unbelievers should have the confidence, when they invite such unbelievers to come to church with them, that they will not be embarrassed by being singled out, but that they will hear God's word clearly proclaimed and, hopefully, be drawn by the Spirit into the family of God.

Our worship services should be carried out in such a manner that all visitors, believers and unbelievers alike, leave with the deep impression "that God was really among [them]" (v. 25).

### Personal Response

1. *What is the difference between the gifts of tongues and prophecy? How do each relate to building the individual? To building the church?*

2. *Have Christians developed our own brand of "tongues" with our spiritual language (vv. 22-26)? How can we explain our Christian faith to unbelievers in language which they can understand?*
3. *How does God speak to individuals today and help them speak to the church in a prophetic way?*
4. *What causes unbelievers to say, "God is among you" (v. 25)?*

# CHAPTER TWENTY-TWO

## Worship in the Early Church

*What then shall we say, brothers? When you come together, everyone has a hymn, or a word of instruction, a revelation, a tongue or an interpretation. All of these must be done for the strengthening of the church. If anyone speaks in a tongue, two — or at the most three — should speak, one at a time, and someone must interpret. If there is no interpreter, the speaker should keep quiet in the church and speak to himself and God.*

*Two or three prophets should speak, and the others should weigh carefully what is said. And if a revelation comes to someone who is sitting down, the first speaker should stop. For you can all prophesy in turn so that everyone may be instructed and encouraged. The spirits of prophets are subject to the control of prophets. For God is not a God of disorder but of peace.*

*As in all the congregations of the saints, women should remain silent in the churches. They are not allowed to speak, but must be in submission, as the Law says. If they want to inquire about something, they should ask their own husbands at home; for it is disgraceful for a woman to speak in the church. Did the word of God originate with you? Or are you the only people it has reached?*

*If anybody thinks he is a prophet or spiritually gifted, let him acknowledge that what I am writing to you is the Lord's command. If he ignores this, he himself will be ignored.*

*Therefore, my brothers, be eager to prophesy, and do not forbid*

*speaking in tongues. But everything should be done in a fitting and orderly way (I
Corinthians 14:26-40).*

To be in Christ is to be in fellowship with other Christians.
Private Christianity is not known in the New Testament; the Christian life is lived in company with others. At the heart of this new
corporate existence in Christ stands the worship of the Christian
community. Here prayer is made, the bread is broken, the saints
are instructed and equipped for their tasks which they must perform when scattered in the world.

The forms of worship in the early church were largely carried
over from the synagogue, although in this area also, the old
wineskins could not contain the new wine. The Spirit of the risen
Lord gave the early believers the freedom to create new forms as
well.

From the few and very brief descriptions of early Christian
worship we get the impression that they were characterized by
great spontaneity. Meetings in private homes would provide the
setting for this freedom on the part of those in attendance. That
such meetings could get a bit chaotic upon occasion stands to
reason.

In our passage Paul seeks to regulate the meetings of the
believers. He does not squelch the spontaneity, but he is concerned
about the upbuilding of the church and the orderliness that such a
purpose demands.

When they come together, says Paul, they should come prepared
to make their individual contributions to the service. One might
have a hymn, another a lesson, a third a revelation, a fourth a
tongue or an interpretation. The expression "each one has" probably means that the different members of the congregation,
depending on their gift, make their individual contributions to the
edification of the church. This should, however, not be read to
mean that every person in the meeting had to say something.

Not only was there spontaneity in early Christian worship, but
also variety. Paul lists five different items here (v. 26), but this can
hardly be an exhaustive list, for nothing is said, for example, of the
Eucharist, the collecting of monies for the poor, the reading of the
Scriptures, and so forth.

A "psalm" might refer to an Old Testament Psalm, but since

the word also means to sing, the reference may be to a Christian composition. The "lesson" refers to a word of instruction from a Christian teacher. Teachers are often listed with prophets (cf. 12:28f) and the "revelation" here probably refers to a prophetic utterance. Then there is the speaking in tongues with the accompanying interpretation.

In all this spontaneity, variety and participation of the congregation, there must always be one over-riding concern: the up-building of all those present. Not ego-trips but the strengthening of the church is the purpose of Christian worship. Since that is so, certain rules of propriety and order must be observed.

### I. Place of Tongues and Prophecy (I Cor. 14:27-33a)

(a) *Regulating glossolalia* (vv. 27, 28). Since the gift of tongues is a gracious gift from God, it cannot be banned entirely from the meetings of the saints. It must be exercised, however, in keeping with the fundamental purpose of the church's worship: for up-building. To achieve that purpose Paul lays down three conditions for the exercise of tongues.

(i) Only two persons may speak in tongues during one service, at the most three. The conditional sentence, "If any speak in a tongue," implies that there need not be any speaking in tongues at all, but if there is, then at the most three people might speak. This restriction would prevent glossolalia from getting out of hand.

(ii) Also, these two or three who may speak in tongues must do so by turns. If they spoke at the same time they would introduce confusion into the worship service. Quite incidentally this indicates that the gift of tongues was completely under the control of the speaker. He would await his turn.

(iii) There is, however, to be no speaking in tongues where there is no interpretation. Paul has explained earlier that what is not understood does not edify, and since people can't understand what is said by the person speaking in tongues in public, those who have this gift may exercise it in private in their devotional life but not in public when it is not understood.

(b) *Regulating prophecy* (vv. 29-33a). Prophets too must observe the rules of propriety. Interestingly, Paul does not say, as in the case of tongues, "if any one prophecies." He assumes that there always will be a prophetic word when the congregation meets.

Again, only two or three prophets should speak at one meeting. We should not think of these prophetic utterances in terms of three half-hour sermons prepared in advance, but rather of extemporaneous discourses on how to live the Christian life according to the will of God.

The value of hearing two or three prophets is that the spiritual diet of the congregation is a bit more balanced than when only one pastor preaches all the time.

Even when two or three prophets instruct the church, the congregation is not to be passive. The hearers are to weigh what is being said. A parallel to this would be I Thessalonians 5:20, 21, "Do not despite prophesying, but test everything." However, it is possible that the "others" who are to listen critically to the prophet who speaks are the other prophets or those who have the gift of discernment (12:10).

Christian etiquette is to be observed by prophets. If, for example, God reveals something to one who is sitting and listening, then the one speaking is to desist and allow his fellow prophet to speak. How he would know when to stop is not stated. Perhaps the one who wished to speak would rise or raise his hand. Clearly no one speaker was to dominate the session.

"For you can all prophecy one by one" is probably a reference to those in the congregation who have the gift of prophecy and not to every last member of the church. Women too had this gift, as 11:4f. indicates.

Again the purpose of gathering for worship is indicated: "So that all may learn and all be encouraged" (v. 31). Church services are not designed to give people with spiritual gifts opportunity to exercise them, but to instruct the believers. Every church service is to be a learning experience.

Those who have been in the church for a long time may think that there is little left to be learned about the Bible or the Christian life. Moreover, the gospel has been given to us once for all and may not be constantly revised and changed. However, this old Word of God can be proclaimed in so many different ways and applied to constantly changing life situations that it remains perennially "fresh" (even if not "new"). Instruction is tied together with *paraklesis* (exhortation, comfort, encouragement) in our text. Teaching the Scriptures is not simply an academic exercise; it aims at the edification of the hearers.

Under the superintendence of the Spirit the prophets (like those with the gift of tongues) are in full control of the use of their gift. "The spirits of the prophets are subject to the prophets" (v. 32). No thought here of prophesying under an uncontrollable impulse! Prophets can speak or be silent, depending on the need of the occasion.

Such regulations for the exercise of tongues and prophecy were given by the apostle to minimize the potential for chaos when the Corinthian church met. Their meetings are to reflect the character of God who is not "a God of confusion, but of peace" (v. 33a). The gathering of the church in the presence of God is not to be characterized by commotion, disorder and chaos.

## II. Place of the Christian Women (I Cor. 14:33b-36)

The new freedom in Christ which believing women received through the gospel seems to have been abused in Corinth. This is obvious from the fact that some even refused to wear the traditional head covering — a violation of the law of propriety for which Paul censures them (I Cor. 11).

In chapter 11 Paul does not put any strictures on the women as far as their participation in Christian worship goes, as long as they do not overstep the bounds of decency. In our passage, however, Paul puts certain restrictions on the women. Evidently they were taking their newly-found freedom too far, and so Paul asks them to be silent in church. "As in all churches of the saints, the women should keep silent in the churches."

In 11:16 Paul speaks of "the churches of God," here of "the churches of the saints." The saints are, of course, the people of God, and so the two expressions may be viewed as interchangeable. It is worth noticing, once again (cf. 11:16), that Paul wants churches to manifest unity not only in doctrine, but also in worship practices. He doesn't want Corinth to strike out *de novo.*

What makes Paul's command for the women to be silent so problematic is not simply that it doesn't seem to fit into our Western culture (although God's Word must always be understood and applied in a cultural context) but rather that it seems to contradict what Paul said in chapter 11. There a woman who observes the laws of propriety in dress is free to pray and prophecy; here she is told not to speak.

How can we harmonize chapter 11 with our passage? The following ways have been suggested. (i) Chapter 11 has the worship service in mind, chapter 14 a business meeting; or, chapter 11 refers to the informal meetings of the church and chapter 14 to the formal. However, we know of no such distinctions in the early church. (ii) That the silence which Paul commands here refers only to speaking in tongues and not to prayer and prophecy. Women speaking in tongues would have added to the confusion at Corinth, and this view should not be ruled out. (iii) That silence applies to the habit of women asking questions during the worship service and not to prayer or prophecy, is another way of reading the text. Very likely men and women sat segregated and wives would have disturbed the service by asking their husbands questions. This view gets support from the advice that if they have questions they should ask their husbands at home. (iv) Since women did not go to school in those days, they would be poorly equipped to speak to the congregation. Some scholars think that once that situation changes (i.e.,once the woman has something to say) Paul's command also falls to the ground. (v) Still others are of the opinion that Paul had to make this restriction only because of the patriarchal culture of his day. Where a culture gives the woman full freedom to speak in public, the church should also allow her that freedom. But, as we read the text carefully, there seems to be something permanent about Paul's instruction.

"For they are not permitted to speak, but should be subordinate, as even the law says" (v. 34). Presumably this is a reference to the creation account where woman was made to be man's helper, "fit for him," and the headship of man was established, as 11:3 states it. Some think "the law" which ordains that the woman shall be subject to her husband refers to Genesis 3:16 where it is stated that the husband, after the Fall, would rule over his wife, taking advantage of her desire for him. But this is not at all certain.

The submission of the wife to her husband is clearly taught in the Scriptures. This should not be thought of as demeaning or galling, for the church voluntarily submits to Christ out of love, and that serves as the model for marriage relationship according to Paul (Eph. 5:21ff.). It is a relationship rooted in creation and hallowed by redemption for the welfare, dignity and honor of both man and woman.

By refraining from speaking in public (speaking in tongues? asking questions? disregarding their husbands' headship?) better order would be established in the Corinthian church. Precisely what the Corinthian women were doing to contribute to the disorder at Corinth is not stated but Paul thought it was shameful (v. 35). However, Paul does not want the women to be spiritually impoverished by desisting from public speaking. (The charge that Paul was a woman hater must be rejected out of hand, for no apostle did so much for the liberation of womanhood as did Paul; cf. Gal. 3:28). Paul wants the Christian woman to be fully informed and to share in all the blessings of salvation. It is striking that precisely in the two passages where Paul counsels the women to be silent (I Cor. 14;I Tim. 2) he wants her to "learn." She shall not be spiritually short-changed because of her sex but shall enjoy the riches of redemption with her husband.

Just as in the matter of dress, so in the matter of a woman's participation in public worship, the Corinthians are warned not to be a law unto themselves as if the word of God first went forth from Corinth or came only to Corinth. In fact it came from Jerusalem. But, be that as it may, the Corinthians are to fall in line with the practices of other Christian churches.

That the command for women to be silent in church cannot be absolutized and universalized is obvious from the New Testament itself where women played an important role in the worship and mission of the church. On the other hand, our passage should not be viewed simply as a prohibition to overcome a local, temporary problem, and which, therefore, has nothing to say to us today. To ordain women to the pastoral leadership of churches is, in our opinion, not in keeping with biblical teaching.

### III. Place for Decency and Order (I Cor. 14:37-40)

Paul has no doubt in his mind that God has guided him in his instruction regarding worship in the church. Yet he anticipates some objectives particularly from those who had the prophetic gift and perhaps also had the gift of tongues (v. 37). The hallmark of true spirituality, Paul argues, is to recognize that what he is writing is in keeping with the teachings of Jesus. Those who have spiritual gifts are not to be a law to themselves, but are to conform to the law of Christ as seen in the apostle's directions.

He who does not recognize Paul's teachings as authoritative is simply not recognized (by Paul? by the church? by Christ?) as a spiritual person.

In keeping with the argument of the entire chapter Paul's summary conclusion is that they should earnestly desire to prophesy because of the benefits the church derives from such an exercise. At the same time it should be recognized that tongues also are a gift of the Spirit and should not be forbidden. The conditions for the exercise of glossolalia have been laid down in the preceding paragraphs.

The over-riding concern in the use of the *charismata* should be to build the church. In order that this may be achieved, there is another principle which applies to the church's meetings at all times: "All things should be done decently and in order" (v. 40).

This principle should not be used to block every effort to revitalize Christian worship or to make innovations. Moreover, what is "proper" (*euschemonos* — good form) and good order will depend to some degree on what is considered appropriate in a given culture. And the order of worship in New Testament times can hardly serve as a model for us when we prepare church bulletins. Moreover, the concern to do things "decently and in order" should not lead us to squelch all spontaneity in public worship.

Naturally, where a congregation is large, the spontaneous element will have to be reduced and other structures may have to be created to allow for greater freedom of expression. How blest are those who can worship in a congregation where spiritual vitality is combined with decorum and good form!

### Personal Response

1. *Worship in the early church had several elements (v. 26). Think back to the last worship service you attended. What was helpful in building you up? What could have been added that would have encouraged you in your faith?*

2. *In the early church, several speakers shared (vv. 29-31). What is the value of having guest speakers or a multiple pulpit ministry in the church? What are the dangers?*

3. *How much have we/should we allow(ed) our culture to guide what*

we do in our worship services?
4. How do we keep balance between spontaneity and order in our worship services?

# CHAPTER TWENTY-THREE

## The Gospel of the Resurrection

*Now, brothers, I want to remind you of the gospel I preached to you, which you received and on which you have taken your stand. By this gospel you are saved, if you hold firmly to the word I preached to you. Otherwise, you have believed in vain.*

*For what I received I passed on to you as of first importance: that Christ died for our sins according to the Scriptures, that he was buried, that he was raised on the third day according to the Scriptures, and that he appeared to Peter, and then to the Twelve. After that, he appeared to more than five hundred of the brothers at the same time, most of whom are still living, though some have fallen asleep. Then he appeared to James, then to all the apostles, and last of all he appeared to me also, as to one abnormally born.*

*For I am the least of the apostles and do not even deserve to be called an apostle, because I persecuted the church of God. But by the grace of God I am what I am, and his grace to me was not without effect. No, I worked harder than all of them — yet not I, but the grace of God that was with me. Whether, then, it was I or they, this is what we preach, and this is what you believed.*

*But if it is preached that Christ has been raised from the dead, how can some of you say that there is no resurrection of the dead? If there is no resurrection of the dead, then not even Christ has been raised. And if Christ has not been raised, our preaching is useless and so is your faith. More than that, we are then found to be false witnesses about God, for we have testified about God that he raised Christ from the dead. But he did not raise him if in fact the dead are not raised. For if the dead are not raised, then Christ has not been raised either. And if Christ has not been raised, your faith is futile; you are still in your sins. Then those also who have fallen asleep in Christ are lost. If only for this life we have hope in Christ, we are to be pitied more than all men.*

*But Christ has indeed been raised from the dead, the firstfruits of those who have fallen asleep. For since death came through a man, the resurrection of the dead comes also through a man. For as in Adam all die, so in Christ all will be made alive. But each in his own turn: Christ, the firstfruits; then, when he comes those who belong to him. Then the end will come, when he hands over the kingdom to God the Father after he has destroyed all dominion, authority and power. For he must reign until he has put all his enemies under his feet. The last enemy to be destroyed is death. For he "has put everything under his feet." Now when it says that "everything" has been put under him, it is clear that this does not include God himself, who put everything under Christ. When he has done this, then the Son himself will be made subject to him who put everything under him, so that God may be all in all (I Corinthians 15:1-28).*

Perhaps there is no letter in the New Testament that treats such a variety of topics in so orderly a manner as does I Corinthians. A brief overview of the ground covered in this epistle may be in place, as we begin our study of this great doctrinal chapter.

In chapters 1-6 Paul dealt with four major problems in the Corinthian congregation — party strife (chaps. 1-4), immorality (chap. 5), law courts (chap. 6:1-11) and libertinism (chap. 6:12-20). With chapter 7 Paul began to answer some of the questions the Corinthians had asked concerning marriage and celibacy (chap. 7) and concerning the eating of meat offered to idols (chaps. 8-10). It may be that Paul's readers had asked him also about the exercise of spiritual gifts. In any case, Paul deals with disorders in public worship in chapters 11-14 — the head covering (chap. 11:1-16), the Lord's Supper (chap. 11:17-34), and the use of spiritual gifts (chaps. 12-14).

Whether the Corinthains had addressed questions on the resurrection to Paul is not known. this long chapter (chap 15) does not begin as do dome of the others, with "now concerning." Paul must have heard that some Corinthians were denying the resurrection and since this doctrine is so fundamental to the Christian faith, he deals with the subject in some detail.

In the Greek world of thought the resurrection of the dead was not a congenial teaching. When Paul preached this doctrine in Athens his hearers laughed him to scorn. Some thought he was preaching foreign deities "because he preached Jesus and the resurrection" (Acts 17:18). (They may have thought that *Anastasis* (resurrection) was the female consort of Jesus, the male deity; apparently Jesus and Anastasis were the strange deities.) Professor Ladd writes: "The idea of personal immortality would have caused no offense to Greeks, but the idea of bodily resurrection was not a truth they could easily accept" ( The Last Things, p. 81).

In the Jewish world the resurrection from the dead was a well known doctrine, but not every Jew accepted it. While belief in the resurrection had received considerable impetus from the martyrdoms under Antiochus Epiphanes, there was still a great deal of controversy about it in the days of Jesus. The Samaritans denied the resurrection of the body, as did the Sadducees (Mt. 12:8-27). The Pharisees held to the resurrection of the dead, but there was considerable debate among the rabbis on whether only the righteous (i.e., Israelites) would be raised, or whether those buried outside the Holy Land would take part in this resurrection, and so forth.

In Paul's gospel the resurrection is at the very center, as we can see from the following paragraphs.

## I. Centrality of the Resurrection (15:1-4)

Paul begins with a mild rebuke: "Now I make known to you, brethren, the gospel which I preached to you." They knew the gospel; they had received it; it was the foundation of their Christian life; but, Paul has to go over it once more (v. 1). We never outgrow the basic teachings of the gospel and need to be reminded of them again and again.

In some letters of Paul we are told that we are saved by "faith," or by "grace"; here we are told that we are saved by the "gospel." The word "saved" (delivered, rescued) is in the present tense, to indicate that our salvation experience had its beginning when we responded to the gospel in faith, but that it is an ongoing experience. In fact, salvation will not be complete until we reach the world to come indicate that our salvation experience had its beginning when we responded to the gospel in faith, but that it is an ongoing experience. In fact, salvation will not be complete until we reach the world to come.

The apostle attaches a condition to their salvation experience — "if you hold fast" (v. 2). If they carried their denial of the resurrection of the body to its logical conclusion they would have believed in vain. The gospel does not work mechanically or magically; there must be a human response to the gospel. The apostles warn repeatedly against the danger of falling away from the faith.

Paul had received the outline of the gospel which he had preached in Corinth from others. That Jesus was alive he had learned directly from heaven on the Damascus road but the historical details of Jesus' life and teachings and passion he got from eyewitnesses, such as Peter (cf. Gal. 1:18). In this gospel message the resurrection was central, for without it Christ's death would have been in vain. Because Christ rose from the dead his death and burial are also of greatest significance and belong to the core of the gospel message (v. 3).

Three important aspects of Jesus' death are (i) that it was Christ, the Messiah, who died — a truth foreign to Jewish expectations; (ii) that he died "for our sins." That Jesus died under Pontius Pilate can be known from secular history, but only the gospel informs us that it was not for some crime he had committed that he died, but that his death atoned "for our sins," (iii) that he died "in accordance with the Scriptures." Paul probably thought of Christ as the Suffering Servant of Isaiah 53 and so he can say that Christ died according to the Scriptures.

Special mention is made of the burial of Jesus, for it stresses not only the finality of his death, but also the reality of the resurrection which followed. This resurrection occurred "on the third day in accordance with the Scriptures" (v. 4). The third day, by inclusive reckoning, was the first day of the week, later called Sunday. Paul may have had Isaiah 53:10b,11 in mind when he wrote that Christ was raised according to the Scriptures. Whether he thought that the Scriptures also predicted the detail about his being raised on the third day is not quite certain. Could Paul have had Leviticus 23:10ff. in mind, where the presentation of the first fruits is prescribed for "the morrow after the sabbath," i.e. following Passover?

What we have in these verses is an early confession of faith in which the fundamental truths of the gospel are spelled out. From this creedal statement Paul goes on to list the witnesses to the resurrection of Jesus in order to dispel any lingering doubts about this historical event in the minds of his readers.

## II. Witnesses to the Resurrection (15:5-11)

The primacy of Peter as a witness to the resurrection reflects his status in the early church. (He also heads the lists of the apostles given in the Gospels and Acts.) Paul regularly uses Peter's Aramaic nickname, Cephas, which means "rock." There was a certain poignancy about the risen Christ's appearance to Peter, since this "pillar apostle" had so shamefully denied his Lord.

The "twelve" also bore evidence to the reality of Christ's resurrection (v. 5). Judas was no longer alive when Christ appeared to his disciples, but the number "twelve" becomes a technical word for the apostolic band. As there were 12 patriarchs, so Christ chose 12 disciples to be the founding fathers of the church, the new people of God.

"Then he appeared to more than five hundred brethren at one time" (v. 6). We have no information on this appearance from the Gospels but Paul no doubt got his information from a Jerusalem source (cf. Gal. 1:18). "Brothers" is normally used in the sense of "Christians" in the NT, but here probably men only are meant. That Paul mentions no women witnesses to the resurrection may be explained by the fact that their testimony in court at that time was of no account.

Since the resurrection took place only some 25 years before Paul wrote this letter, it is not surprising that most of these, as Paul says, were still alive, although some had "fallen asleep" (i.e. died). The fact that so many were still alive and could be called in as witnesses gave strong credibility to Christ's resurrection.

The Gospels omit the living Christ's appearance to James, the Lord's brother, and the apocryphal gospels fill this gap with interesting details. Like his other brothers, James was, to begin with, an unbeliever (cf. Jn. 7:5), but the resurrection of Jesus changed all that.

Finally Christ appeared to all the apostles (v. 7). This is obviously a larger number than the twelve. To this wider circle of apostles belongs also Paul.

"Last of all he appeared to me as to one untimely born" (v. 8). As Paul saw it, his vision of the risen Christ on the Damascus road was of the same order as the appearances he has just listed. To Paul's knowledge no one after him had been granted such an appearance of the risen Lord and so he can say "last of all...to me." And since he was made an apostle when he was persecuting the church in his unbelief, he calls himself an "abortion." This may refer to the violent manner in which he came into the kingdom, or it may point to Paul's unsightly appearance, or else, his enemies who questioned his apostleship called him an "abortion" of an apostle.

Humbly he acknowledges that he is "the least of the apostles, unfit to be called an apostle" (v. 9), as he remembers the violence with which he treated God's church before his conversion. The forgiving grace of God had pulled the sting out of this awful memory, but Paul never forgot his past misdeeds and the memory of them gave him an understanding for the grace of God few others have had.

And so he confesses joyously, "but by the grace of God I am what I am, and his grace toward me was not in vain" (v. 10). As a late comer to the apostolate he made up for lost time by working harder than others. Within the span of a few years he had planted the gospel in Galatia, Macedonia and Achaia, and at the moment was evangelizing Asia. All the credit, of course, goes to the grace of God which was with him.

But, whatever the comparative importance of the apostles, they all preach the same gospel (v. 11). Peter, James and others proclaim the message of the resurrection just as Paul does. The gospel to the Jews, entrusted to Peter, was no different from the gospel to the Gentiles, entrusted to Paul (Gal. 2:7f.).

The resurrection of Jesus from the dead guarantees the resurrection of all the dead. The Corinthians evidently had not made this connection and so Paul will show them where a denial of the resurrection of the dead leads.

### III. Denial of the Resurrection (15:12-19)

There is no evidence that any of the Corinthians denied Christ's resurrection, but there was doubt about the resurrection of the dead (v. 12). Paul argues that you can't believe in one without the other (v. 13). A denial of the resurrection of the dead, driven to its logical conclusion, implies a denial of Christ's resurrection. And if the latter is denied, then the preaching of the apostles is an empty sham, as is also the faith of those who believed his gospel (v. 14).

Moreover, the apostles are then guilty of misrepresenting God by testifying that he raised Christ from the dead when in fact he did not (v. 15).

Repeating the arugment of verses 12-14, Paul underscores the close connection between Christ's resurrection and the resurrection of the dead. To deny the latter implies a denial of the former (v. 16). And if Christ's resurrection were not an historical fact, then their faith would be futile; "you are still in your sins" (v. 17). It was by the resurrection that the power of sin was broken, and if Christ had not risen, the Corinthians would still be in bondage to sin.

And not only that, but they would have no hope of eternal life. All those who fell asleep (i.e. died) in Christ, confident that he would raise them up in the last day, died deceived and without hope, forever cut off from God (v. 18).

Moreover, Paul argues that hope in Christ has benefits for this present life. Christian hope rests on the resurrection of Jesus Christ, and if he is not risen "then we are all men most to be pitied" (v. 19). All our labor for Christ, all our sacrifices, would be a hollow mockery if Christ were not alive. To deny Christ's resurrection is to destroy the very foundation on which the Christian life is built.

Five reasons why we should be a miserable lot if there were no resurrection are: (i) preaching is in vain; (ii) the apostles are liars; (iii) faith is futile; (iv) sin's power is not broken; (v) there is no hope for the future.

## IV. Significance of the Resurrection (15:20-28)

Turning from the terrible conclusions which must accompany the denial of the resurrection, Paul now enumerates the glorious consequences of Christ's resurrection. The evidences for the resurrection of Christ are so overwhelming that Paul breaks off contemplating the tragic condition of mankind if Christ were still in the grave. "But in fact Christ has been raised from the dead, the firstfruits of those who have fallen asleep" (v. 20). The firstfruits are the guarantee that the harvest will follow. The feast of firstfruits followed immediately upon Passover and inaugurated the seven weeks which ended with Pentecost. Paul may have been writing this letter between Passover (cf. 5:7f) and Pentecost (16:8), and the metaphor of the firstfruits may have been very much in his mind. If Christ (the firstfruits) was raised, the harvest (mankind's resurrection) must of necessity follow.

Paul now proceeds to draw an analogy between the representative men: Adam, the head of the old creation, Christ, the head of the new. By Adam came the fall and death as punishment for man's rebellion; by Christ, the new Adam, comes the resurrection from the dead (v. 21). "As in Adam all die, so also in Christ shall all be made alive" (v. 22). Although Paul focuses primarily on the future resurrection of the believers in this chapter, Christ's resurrection guarantees the resurrection of all mankind — the former for eternal life, the latter for eternal ruin.

But each will be raised in his own order (*tagma* is a military word, suggesting companies appearing in their proper position). First is the resurrection of Christ, the firstfruits, then those who belong to Christ, who will be raised at the *parousia* (the technical word in the NT for Christ's glorious advent) (v. 23). That there was to be an interval between Christ's resurrection and the resurrection of all believers at his coming is taught elsewhere by Paul.

After the resurrection of the saints at Christ's return comes the end of this age, the termination of this world-order. Some have argued that the end (*telos*) refers to the resurrection of the dead who did not die in Christ (cf. Rev. 20:5) but this is doubtful.

When the end comes (v. 24) then Christ will deliver "the kingdom to God the Father, after destroying every rule and every authority and power." The kingship of Christ, the age of Messiah, began with his exaltation to the right hand of God. This kingly reign, however, is still opposed by evil powers. Nevertheless, in the end all these opposing forces will have to yield and Christ will be all in all.

Christ's reign over evil powers began when he was exalted to the right hand of God (using the language of Ps. 110:1) and this reign continues in the present until God has "put all his enemies under his feet" (v. 25). This is an oriental metaphor for the complete subjugation of an opposing force to the victorious conqueror.

One stubborn enemy, however, refuses to yield during the time when the church waits for Christ's return. "The last enemy to be destroyed is death" (v. 26). The decisive battle in the war with evil powers, including death, was fought when Christ died and rose triumphantly from the grave on that first Christian Easter. But we must wait a while before the victory becomes fully obvious.

Because of his victory at the cross and the resurrection, "God has put all things in subjection under his feet." This quotation from Psalm 8:6 refers originally to man's lordship over creation, but here it applies to Christ's lordship over all that terrain which was lost because of Adam's sin. "All things" under Christ's feet, Paul is careful to note, does not mean that God also is subject to Christ (v. 27). Christ's unlimited dominion in no way impinges on the Father's sovereignty.

Once Christ has brought this whole estranged creation under God's control, he will have accomplished his mediatorial ministry and will give his kingdom, which he obtained by his death and resurrection, over to the Father. "Then the Son himself will be subjected to him who put all things under him, that God may be all in all" (v. 28). That there is no rivalry between the Son and the Father is clear from the fact that the Father puts all things under his Son's feet. The Son, having completed his redemptive mission, which took him into the depth of his incarnation and passion, hands the reigns of authority over to the Father. The stamp of that humble submissiveness, by which the Son obtained dominion over all opposing powers, will characterize the kingdom of God in the ages to come.

A little break in a dyke in the Netherlands may be insignificant to begin with, but eventually the North Sea will rush into the land. Similarly, as Karl Heim puts it, "Christ's death was but a crack in the vast prison house of death; but the hour will come when the gates of death will yield, our last enemy will lie prostrate, and we will be raised to eternal life with God. By that hope we live."

### Personal Response

*1. I Corinthians 15:3-4 gives some of what Paul felt important to be included in a statement of faith. Write your own confession of faith, listing those things which you feel are important to believe and do.*

2. *The resurrected Christ appeared to Paul and numerous other eye-witnesses (vv. 5-7). How is Christ appearing to you in your present life?*
3. *What are the effects of the resurrection of Christ on a) our personal salvation, b) the church, c) Satan, and d) creation?*
4. *What message does a believer have for an unbelieving world if Christ is not risen?*

# CHAPTER TWENTY-FOUR

## "And I Will Raise Him Up at the Last Day"

*Now if there is no resurrection, what will those do who are baptized for the dead? If the dead are not raised at all, why are people baptized for them? And as for us, why do we endanger ourselves every hour? I die every day — I mean that, brothers — just as surely as I glory over you in Christ Jesus our Lord. If I fought wild beasts in Ephesus for merely human reasons, what have I gained? If the dead are not raised, "Let us eat and drink, for tomorrow we die." Do not be misled: "Bad company corrupts good character." Come back to your senses as you ought, and stop sinning; for there are some who are ignorant of God — I say this to your shame.*

*But someone may ask, "How are the dead raised? With what kind of body will they come?" How foolish! What you sow does not come to life unless it dies. When you sow, you do not plant the body that will be, but just a seed perhaps of wheat or of something else. But God gives it a body as he has determined, and to each kind of seed he gives its own body. All flesh is not the same: Men have one kind of flesh, animals have another, birds another and fish another. There are also heavenly bodies and there are earthly bodies; but the splendor of the heavenly bodies is one kind, and the splendor of the earthly bodies another. The sun has one kind of splendor, the moon another and the stars another; and star differs from star in splendor.*

*So will it be with the resurrection of the dead. The body that is sown is perishable, it is raised imperishable; it is sown in*

187

*dishonor, it is raised in glory; it is sown in weakness, it is raised in power; it is sown a natural body, it is raised a spiritual body.*

*If there is a natural body, there is also a spiritual body. So it is written: "The first man Adam became a living being"; the last Adam, a life-giving spirit. The spiritual did not come first, but the natural, and after that the spiritual. The first man was of the dust of the earth, the second man from heaven. As was the earthly man, so are those who are of the earth; and as is the man from heaven, so also are those who are of heaven. And just as we have borne the likeness of the earthly man, so shall we bear the likeness of the man from heaven. I declare to you, brothers, that flesh and blood cannot inherit the kingdom of God, nor does the perishable inherit the imperishable. Listen, I tell you a mystery: We will not all sleep, but we will all be changed — in a flash, in the twinkling of an eye, at the last trumpet. For the trumpet will sound, the dead will be raised imperishable, and we will be changed. For the perishable must clothe itself with the imperishable, and the mortal with immortality. When the perishable has been clothed with the imperishable, and the mortal with immortality, then the saying that is written will come true: "Death has been swallowed up in victory." "Where, O death, is your victory? Where, O death, is your sting?" The sting of death is sin, and the power of sin is the law. But thanks be to God! He gives us the victory through our Lord Jesus Christ.*

*Therefore, my dear brothers, stand firm. Let nothing move you. Always give yourselves fully to the work of the Lord, because you know that your labor in the Lord is not in vain (I Corinthians 15:29-58).*

The promise of Jesus, repeated four times in John 6 (vv. 39,40,44,54), is a fitting title for what Paul has to say about the resurrection of the dead at the end of the age. I can never read this promise without thinking of the tragic death of my older brother in an air crash in Quebec at 21 years of age. Among his personal effects, sent to us after his death, was a New Testament which otherwise showed no signs that he had been reading it except that this fourfold promise of Jesus, "and I will raise him up in the last day," was underlined. In moments of despair even lines drawn under such promises become symbols of hope.

Paul believed firmly that Christ would fulfill this promise at the last day. His hope of the resurrection was based not only on a sure word of Jesus, but also on an historical event — the resurrection of Jesus. Death, the last enemy to be overcome, continues to do its grisly work, but it received a mortal wound on that Easter morning when our Lord rose from the grave.

Paul has argued in the paragraphs preceding our passage that belief in Christ's resurrection demands belief in the resurrection of all the dead. He will now give a few illustrations of how the hope of the resurrection manifests itself in life.

## I. Expressions of Hope in a Resurrection (15:29-34)

Without endorsing the practice itself, Paul refers to the custom of people "being baptized on behalf of the dead" (v. 29). People surely would not do such strange things if they did not believe in a future resurrection, Paul suggests. Precisely how this practice got started or how deeply the Corinthians were involved in it is not stated. In fact, it is not even known exactly what baptism for the dead means. Did believers get themselves baptized for those who had died (perhaps in an epidemic) and who did not have the chance to get baptized? One can hardly conceive of Corinthians getting baptized vicariously on behalf of unbelieving friends. Or, did some Corinthians accept baptism in order to be reunited with their departed Christian friends in the life to come? The Roman Catholic practice of praying for the dead, commended in 2 Mac. 12:39-45, finds no support in the New Testament.

Whatever the reasons for this practice of proxy baptism, Paul points to it as an argument that people do believe in a resurrection, without condoning or condemning it.

Another practical argument for hope in the resurrection can be found in Paul's own experience. If there were no resurrection then why should he endure dangers and hardships in his service for Christ. "Why am I in peril every hour?" asks the apostle (v. 30). Indeed, he looks death in the face every day (v. 31). And lest there be any doubt in the minds of the readers about this, Paul affirms that what he claims is as certain as is his pride in them. He may criticize the Corinthians for their faults and foibles but he boasts of them to others (cf. II Cor. 1:14, 7:4,14).

"I die daily" is not a reference to his death to self and sin (cf. Rom. 6), but speaks of the dangerous kind of life Paul had to live as servant of Christ. His readiness to die is an expression of his firm grasp of the hope of the resurrection. Paul could afford to risk his life, because he knew that physical death was not the end. Beyond the grave lay an endless life with God.

One example of what Paul meant by dying daily was his experience at Ephesus where he fought with wild beasts (v. 32). This is probably metaphorical language, for Roman citizens were exempt from such treatment. Ignatius (ca. A.D. 110), bishop of Antioch, wrote to the Romans as he was led away to his death that he was tied to leopards (meaning soldiers). Paul evidently had been in mortal danger in Ephesus and he describes his experience as an encounter with wild beasts. Perhaps the reference is to the Demetrius riot (Acts 19:23ff.).

Paul argues that he would not have got himself into such dangerous situations if there were no resurrection and death was the end of all existence. In fact, if the dead did not rise, he might also choose to live by the maxim: "Let us eat and drink for tomorrow we die" (v. 32). This is a quotation from Isaiah 22:13 (but see also Eccl. 2:24) and sums up a reasonable philosophy of life, if there were no resurrection.

Keeping company with people who deny the resurrection, Paul warns, could have a detrimental effect on the Corinthians. "Bad company ruins good morals," is a quote from Menander (ca. 320 B.C.), and may suggest that those readers who doubted the resurrection of the dead tended to take a libertine line on morals (cf. 6:12ff.). Whether Paul had ever read Menander's *Thais* is not known for this may well have been a popular proverb in Paul's day.

No one can question the fact that bad company ruins good morals, and so Paul calls on his readers to sober up and to stop sinning (v. 34). Doctrinal errors tend to lead to serious moral faults. One cannot for long keep one's beliefs in one compartment and one's morals in another. And whereas there were those in Corinth who claimed a deep knowledge of God (perhaps the Gnostics), Paul blames them for their ignorance of God. "To know God" is to live in his presence and to do his will.

From the evidence for the hope of the resurrection and his criticism of those who question it, Paul goes on to answer the question on the nature of the resurrection body.

## II. Nature of the Resurrection Body (15:35-49)

Paul is sure that some of his readers will find it hard to believe in the resurrection and may ask: "How are the dead raised? With what kind of body do they come?" (v. 35). His sharp retort, "You foolish man," suggests that such questions betrayed a basic misunderstanding of the resurrection. If resurrection meant the reanimation of the earthly body buried in the ground, one might well raise objections to this teaching. However, personal identity does not require the reconstitution of our flesh and bones. An analogy will help us to understand what Paul means.

(a) *The Analogy* (vv. 36-41). Before new life can spring from a seed, it has to die. But the plant that springs from this kernel that is put into the ground is very different from the kernel. A naked seed of wheat is put into the ground and from it springs a grass, a stem, an ear of grain (v. 37). Moreover, there is an endless variety of seeds and consequently an endless variety of "bodies" that spring from these seeds (v. 38). God, the Creator, is active in his creation, giving a body to each of the billions of seeds that die in the ground annually. The seed and the plant that springs from it bear little resemblance to each other but there is a continuity between the two. Similarly there is a continuity between what we are today and what we will be in the resurrection even though the resurrection body will be quite different from our earthly bodies.

From grain Paul turns to flesh, to show the great diversity in God's creation order. There is, for example, the flesh of men, of animals, birds and fish (v. 39). In addition to these terrestrial bodies there are celestial bodies as well (v. 40). There is the sun and the moon and the many different kinds of stars (v. 41). Each of these has its appropriate glory or degree of brightness. Infinite variety characterizes God's creation. That being so, we should surely not question God's ability to give us new bodies after our earthly frame has gone to the dust.

(b) *The Application* (vv. 42-49). Just as the plant is different from the seed that is sown, so the resurrection body will differ from this body of flesh and blood. "What is sown is perishable, what is raised is imperishable" (v. 42). In contrast to our bodies of flesh and blood, which are sown in the ground and return to the dust at death, the resurrection body is immortal; it is not subject to death and corruption.

There is no honor in having our bodies wracked with pain and distorted by disease and finally to have them lowered into a hole in the ground. It is rather a sign of abject weakness. But, says Paul, they will be raised in glory and in power (v. 43).

The body that is lowered into the grave at death is a "physical" body. The Greek adjective *psychikos* (a "soulish" body) was very likely suggested to Paul by the creation account, in which man became "a living soul" in the hands of the Creator (Gen. 2:7). The body that will be raised is described as a "spiritual" body (v. 44). "Spiritual" does not mean invisible, intangible, ethereal, but a body under the sway of the Spirit of God. The contrast between these two kinds of bodies is like that of the first to the last Adam. The first Adam became a living being, the last, namely Christ, became a life-giving Spirit (v. 45). Christ's resurrection body is so possessed by the Spirit that he shares his life giving powers with us, even now. "If the Spirit of him who raised Jesus from the dead dwells in you, he who raised Christ Jesus from the dead will give life to your mortal bodies also through the Spirit which dwells in you (Roman 8:11).

In God's ordering of history the physical body of Adam came first, the spiritual body of the risen Christ came later (v. 46). The first man, Adam, was a man of dust from the ground (as Gen. 2:7 puts it); the second man, the risen Christ, is from heaven (v. 47) and, therefore, has a heavenly body. At present, here on earth, our mortal bodies are like Adam's, dust of the ground. In the future, however, at the resurrection, they will partake of the heavenly nature of Christ's resurrection body (v. 48). As descendants of Adam we all bear his image in our bodies which, like his, return to the dust; but the day will come when we will "bear the image of the man from heaven" (v. 49), for, as Paul says elsewhere, he "will change our lowly body to be like his glorious body, by the power which enables him even to subject all things to himself" (Phil. 3:21).

There is a difference, then, between a "bodily" resurrection (which Paul clearly teaches) and a "physical" resurrection, a resurrection of relics, which is not taught in the Bible. We needn't be troubled, therefore, about John Wycliffe's resurrection body, even though his remains were burned to ashes and scattered on the River Swift. He will have a new body.

Dr. William Temple, trying desperately to keep up with his friends as they climbed a hill but constantly falling behind, broke out in the profound confession: "Thank God I do not believe in the resurrection of the flesh." He did believe in the resurrection of the body, but he had the hope that his resurrection body would be different in nature from the one he now had. This body will be glorious and that should lay to rest all fears that the "spiritual" body is of lesser value than our present bodies. Mr. Boothby was all mixed up when he remarked that a "spiritual Mr. Boothby, twanging a spiritual harp for all eternity had little attraction for him." A spiritual body means that our personalities will be completely possessed by the Spirit of God. To enter upon such a heavenly existence our bodies need to be transformed.

### III. Transformation of the Body at the Resurrection
### (15:50-57)

"I tell you this, brethren: flesh and blood cannot inherit the kingdom of God, nor does the perishable inherit the imperishable" (v. 50). "Flesh and blood" describes our earthly, mortal body. It is a body perfectly suited to life in this world, a body that should be treated with respect and dignity. But this body is ill-suited for the world to come. "The kingdom of God" in our passage refers to the future dimension of that reign of God which was inaugurated by the coming of Jesus. To "inherit" this kingdom means to enter it some time in the future when the present age comes to an end. That future kingdom is a spiritual realm which is not characterized by mortality as in our present existence, and so, in order to enter that kingdom in the future, our bodies of flesh and blood have to be transformed.

John Baillie wrote so perceptively, "Nobody ever wanted an endless quantity of life until discovery had been made of a new and quite particular quality of life." This life was made possible by Christ, the life-giving Spirit.

If anyone should ask how Paul got to know that our bodies would some day be transformed, his answer is that it was revealed to him by God. "Behold, I tell you a mystery" (v. 51). A mystery is something hidden in God that has now been made known. Moreover, Paul has been given an added insight. Not only will the bodies of those who have died be raised at the resurrection, but the bodies of the saints alive at Christ's coming will also be transformed.

"We shall not all sleep, but we shall all be changed." A number of manuscripts read "we shall all sleep," but the omission of the "not" probably arose out of the attempt to save Paul from embarrassment after he had in fact fallen asleep (i.e. died). There are other variants, but our text is the most widely attested and best explains the variants that have arisen from it. Codex Beza reads "we shall not all be changed," and Tertullian interpreted that to mean that only the living (not the dead) needed to be changed (the resurrection of the dead, he thought, included their transformation). The best reading, however, has it that all shall be changed, both dead and living.

"This transformation will occur in one moment (*atomos* is that which is indivisible — our word "atom"), "in the twinkling of an eye" (*rhipe* — throwing, casting; the glance of an eye). Our bodies will be changed in a split second when the last trumpet sounds (v. 52).

Jesus said that the trumpet would be blown at his coming to signal the gathering of the elect from "the ends of the earth" (Mt. 24:31). Paul mentions the trumpet as an attendant circumstance of the *Parousia* in I Thessalonians 4:16f. In the Old Testament the trumpet announced the year of jubilee (Lev. 24:9) as well as the annual sabbatical month (Lev. 24:24). Later it came to be associated with the day of the Lord (Zeph. 1:16). The "last" trumpet marks the end of the present order and the inauguration of the age to come. When the last trumpet sounds, that is, when God gives the signal, the dead in Christ shall rise and all the saints will be transformed to the image of Christ's glorious body.

In II Corinthians 5, death is called an "undressing," for in death we put off this body of clay. Conversely, the resurrection and transformation is described as a "dressing" — "for this perishable nature must put on the imperishable, and this mortal nature put on immortality" (v. 54). The verse is an example of synonymous parallelism, although strictly speaking, "immortality" is a more comprehensive term than "imperishable."

In that hour, when we put on the imperishable, immortal body, "then shall come to pass the saying that is written, 'Death is swallowed up in victory'" (v. 54). Paul here quotes Isaiah 25:8 in a version that differs both from the Hebrew and the Septuagint text. In the Isaiah passage God promises that death, which came by the Assyrian conqueror, will be swallowed up; here the reference is to death in general, that last enemy to be overcome.the words "victory" and "death" call forth another Old Testament passage: "O death, where is thy victory? O death, where is thy sting" (Hos. 13:14). In Hosea, Death and Sheol are invited to come and be the executors of God's judgment on Ephraim. Paul treats this double question as a defiant challenge to death to do its worst. In the Byzantine Greek text *hades* (translated by AV as "grave") is found instead of "death" but Paul nowhere else uses the word Hades and prefers to use death twice over.

With "the sting of death" Paul may be personifying death with a goad in its hand to rule and to torture man. Or he may be thinking of some "poisonous tip, so that death is a dangerous beast which gives man a mortal prick" (L. Schmidt, *kentron*, in *TDNT*, III, 668). The apostle goes on to explain that the sting of death is sin (v. 56). Death is seen as God's judgment on sin. The cause of death which the doctor establishes is not, in the thinking of biblical writers, the real cause. Man does not die simply from this or that illness, but because he is a sinner. The reign of death rests on the power of sin, and since sin, as Paul explains in Romans 7:7ff., gains a foothold by means of the law, man is in the clutches of this awesome enemy.

If death is the consequence of sin, then the power of death can be broken only if sin is removed. And since Christ has broken sin's power by his death and resurrection, Paul cannot contain himself; he breaks out in a joyous thanksgiving, "Thanks be unto God who gives us the victory through our Lord Jesus Christ" (v. 57). The present participle ("he keeps on giving") suggests that already in this life we taste that victory which we will experience in all its glory when the reign of death comes to an end at the coming of our Lord.

### IV. Living in the Light of the Resurrection
### (15:58)

With that kind of hope the Corinthians can stand firm and immovable. Threats of torture and even death cannot shake their faith, for they know that death is but the gateway to life.

Moreover, they now have an added incentive to labor with joy for the sake of the kingdom of God for they know that their "labors are not in vain in the Lord" (v. 58). The church is invincible because it shares in an unshakable kingdom. Even the powers of death cannot prevail against it (Mt. 16:18).

The gnawing fear of those without this hope is that some day all that for which they have lived here on earth will be gone. For that reason death is generally camouflaged in our society; one doesn't want to entertain such a morbid subject. The believer can look death squarely in the face with the assurance that when the Grim Reaper has done his worst, the Easter sun beckons him to a glad tomorrow in the presence of God.

### *Personal Response*

1. *If you were to learn that the resurrection of Christ was a hoax, what changes would you make in your personal life?*
2. *Compare and contrast a funeral of a believer and a funeral of an unbeliever. How do people try to camouflage death? What are the results?*
3. *Verses 33-34 tell us not to be misled in our belief or action. Many people in our society do not believe in the resurrection or have no knowledge of what the end of life will be like. How can we maintain a firm belief in the resurrection in such times? How can we witness to such people who will "wait till the end to know what it really will be like"?*
4. *In the resurrection of our bodies, the quality (as well as the quantity) of our lives will be drastically changed. Until that time, what can we do to improve the quality of our physical lives? To what extremes should we go to preserve our physical bodies? What about extreme medical practices?*

# CHAPTER TWENTY-FIVE

## Instructions, Plans and Greetings

*Now about the collection for God's people; Do what I told the Galatian churches to do. On the first day of every week, each one of you should set aside a sum of money in keeping with his income, saving it up, so that when I come no collections will have to be made. Then, when I arrive, I will give letters of introduction to the men you approve and send them with your gift to Jerusalem. If it seems advisable for me to go also, they will accompany me.*

*After I go through Macedonia, I will come to you — for I will be going through Macedonia. Perhaps I will stay with you awhile, or even spend the winter, so that you can help me on my journey, wherever I go. I do not want to see you now and make only a passing visit; I hope to spend some time with you, if the Lord permits. But I will stay on at Ephesus until Pentecost, because a great door for effective work has opened to me, and there are many who oppose me.*

*If Timothy comes, see to it that he has nothing to fear while he is with you, for he is carrying on the work of the Lord, just as I am. No one, then, should refuse to accept him. Send him on his way in peace so that he may return to me. I am expecting him along with the brothers.*

*Now about our brother Apollos: I strongly urged him to go to you with the brothers. He was quite unwilling to go now, but he will go when he has the opportunity.*

*Be on your guard; stand firm in the faith; be men of courage;*
*be strong. Do everything in love.*
 *You know that the household of Stephanas were the first con-*
*verts in Achaia, and they have devoted themselves to the service of*
*the saints. I urge you, brothers, to submit to such as these and to*
*everyone who joins in the work, and labors at it. I was glad when*
*Stephanas, Fortunatus and Achaicus arrived, because they have*
*supplied what was lacking from you. For they refreshed my spirit*
*and yours also. Such men deserve recognition.*
 *The churches in the province of Asia send you greetings. Aquila*
*and Priscilla greet you warmly in the Lord, and so does the church*
*that meets at their house. All the brothers here send you greetings.*
*Greet one another with a holy kiss.*
 *I, Paul, write this greeting in my own hand.*
 *"If anyone does not love the Lord — a curse be on him. Come,*
*O Lord! The Grace of the Lord Jesus be with you. My love to all*
*of you in Christ Jesus (I Corinthians 16:1-24).*

This final chapter of I Corinthians covers such a variety of
topics that it is hard to bring them all under one theme. Our
heading and outline reflect this diversity.

After dealing with a number of current problems at Corinth,
answering some of the church's questions and opening up for us
some of the theological and practical significance of the doctrine of
the resurrection, Paul becomes very personal. He writes about his
travel plans and those of his colleagues; he greets them and sends
along the greetings of friends; he thanks them for sending a delegation to visit him and adds some final words of exhortation.

However harsh Paul's criticisms in this letter may have been,
it is obvious he carries no animosities towards his readers in his
heart. Perhaps we should learn from him how to speak the truth
without failing in love.

The chapter begins with a word of instruction on the collection
for the saints in Jerusalem.

## I. Collection for Jerusalem (16:1-4)

The introductory formula "now concerning" (cf. 7:1) suggest
that the Corinthians may have asked Paul about the collection.
Evidently they had heard that gentile churches were collecting
monies for the poor in Jerusalem to whom all the gentile churches
owed a debt since the gospel had come from Jerusalem to the

Mediterranean world. The gentile Christians are also called "saints" for they had been incorporated as fellow citizens with the original saints (Eph. 2:19).

The word "collection" (*logeia*) occurs only in this passage in the New Testament. Normally Paul uses words such as "grace," "fellowship," "ministry," "generosity," and the like, for the donations of Christians. Such names for the gathering of money for the poor make it clear that practical concerns for the needy are very much a part of the spiritual life of the church. Paul began his own public ministry not by being sent out into the mission field, but by bringing famine relief from Antioch to Jerusalem (Acts 11:30) and he had agreed with the other apostles that in his work among gentiles he would not forget the poor (Gal. 2:10).

The apostle considered the contributions of gentile churches to the Jerusalem church to be very important. Not only did these churches thereby express their gratitude to the "mother church" for sending them the gospel, but it was also a profound demonstration of the unity of the church. Moreover, it also indicated the maturity of the gentile believers, that they were concerned about the poor, as Jesus had been.

There may have been a number of reasons why the Christians in Jerusalem were so poor at this time. Whether they themselves could be blamed for their poverty is not a question for Paul; they were in need and that was reason enough to help.

The apostle had already asked the Galatian churches to contribute to this fund and he mentions that to encourage the Corinthians to take this matter in hand forthwith. Here we have precedent for churches cooperating in relief efforts and we should not fail in this biblical practice.

In order to get some system into the collecting of monies, Paul advises that his readers should lay aside a certain amount on every first day of the week. This is the earliest indication that Christians met on the first day of the week. Sunday by Sunday they were to set aside a portion of their weekly income. Paul doesn't say that they were to bring these gifts to church. Presumably each person was to store them up at home but the practice of bringing gifts for the poor to the church is very old (e.g. Justin, *Apology*, ca. A.D. 155).

Paul suggests that giving be regular and systematic, but also that it be proportionate. "As he may prosper" is in the passive voice and may suggest, "as God has caused him to prosper." We have a more complex economy than people did in Paul's day, but it is a serious violation of biblical practice when wealthy Christians tie all their monies up in investments and then have little to give because they don't get a monthly check as do laborers.

The collected monies were to be taken to Jerusalem by delegates approved by the churches (v. 3). It appears as if Paul wanted to supply the delegates with letters of accreditation. Some of these delegates are listed in Acts 20:4. Notice how careful Paul is in the handling of public church funds. He wants the churches to bring these monies to Jerusalem lest he be suspected of financial irregularities.

If it seems advisable to Paul he will also come to Jerusalem together with them (v. 4). On what Paul's going depended he does not say, but traveling in those days was no picnic and the apostle had to have a good reason to go before he made such a long journey. As it turned out, Paul did go (Rom. 15:25ff.).

## II. Planned Visits (16:5-12)

(a) *Paul's Plans* (vv. 5-9). It is not wrong to make plans, as long as such plans remain flexible. Paul, writing from Ephesus, plans to visit his readers when he comes through Macedonia. As it turned out, Paul apparently paid Corinth a brief and painful visit, travelling by ship, before he made the overland trip via Macedonia (II Cor. 1:15f., 13:1).

At the moment his plan is to come to Corinth for an extended visit, perhaps even to spend the winter with them. From there he plans to make further journeys and hopes his readers will equip him for these travels. However, all his plans are subject to God's will. "If the Lord permits" is written over his travel plans.

It was custom years ago for believers to write D.V. (*deo volente* — "if God wills") after departure dates. Perhaps we needn't write it, but we should certainly have a D.V. in our hearts and minds.

Paul plans to stay in Ephesus at least till Pentecost (as a good Jew he couldn't help but think of the year in terms of the Jewish sacred calendar). Presumably this letter was written around Easter (cf. I Cor. 5:7; 15:20) and that would mean another seven weeks of work in Ephesus (v. 8).

One reason he hesitated to leave Ephesus was the "great and

effective door" that was open to him at the moment (v. 9). The "door" is a metaphor for opportunity. Perhaps it is worth noting that Paul labored where he had opportunity. On several occasions he had to leave unexpectedly because of a closed door. We don't need to be idle just because one door has closed on us; there may be other doors waiting to be entered.

Of one thing we can be sure, however, and that is, wherever there is a fruitful field of ministry, the Devil will be there to oppose God's work. The proverb, "if God builds a chapel, the Devil builds a cathedral across the street," is only too true. Satan knows he has little time and, even though he is a defeated foe, he puts up a fierce struggle as long as this age lasts. Of course, he uses people to oppose God's work — "and there are many adversaries."

(b) *Timothy's Arrival* (vv. 10,11). According to 4:17, Timothy was on the way to Corinth via Macedonia to remind the church of Paul's "ways," i.e. his teachings. Paul expects him to arrive at any time (departure and arrival dates could not then be given with the accuracy with which they are announced today).

Paul's concern is, that when his younger colleague arrives, they receive him kindly, so that he be without fear among them (v. 10). Timothy seems to have been a bit diffident and Paul feared the Corinthians, who had the temptation to be somewhat arrogant and overbearing, would intimidate his youthful emissary. Since Timothy was working for the same Lord as Paul, they had every reason to respect him.

Moreover, the Corinthians are cautioned not to despise Timothy. Perhaps he was still a bit young and some Corinthians might interpret his timidity as weakness. But Paul knew the worth of Timothy and it speaks volumes for the apostle that he would be so solicitous for his younger co-worker.

He wants them to send him on in peace to join Paul and the brothers. Who these brothers were we do not know, but evidently after Timothy returned to Ephesus, Paul sent him and Erastus to Macedonia (Acts 19:22), where he planned to meet them.

(c) *Apollos' Intentions* (v. 12). "Concerning Apollos" suggests that the Corinthians had asked about him. This great orator had a fruitful ministry in Corinth and, without intending to do so, had become a rallying cry for one of the parties in the church. Apollos was presently at Ephesus as well, and Paul had encouraged him again and again to return to Corinth, but Apollos had demurred. (The Greek word for "will" has no article and so it isn't clear whether it was not Apollos' will or God's will, or both.)

Could it be that Apollos did not want to encourage the Apollos party by returning? Paul's relationship to Apollos had not been affected by the party strife in Corinth. Nor was Paul afraid that by returning to Corinth the Apollos party would grow at the expense of the Pauline. Both Paul and Apollos alike were opposed to the party strife in Corinth. That did not mean that Apollos would never again set foot on Corinth, but he would come at an opportune time. Whether he ever returned to visit the Corinthians is not known.

### III. Closing Exhortations (16:13,14)

Paul follows up his information on the planned visits of church leaders with five imperatives; as if to say, regardless of whether I, Timothy, or Apollos come or don't come, "Be watchful, stand firm in the faith, be courageous, be strong. Let all that you do be done in love" (vv. 13,14).

The first two exhortations are defensive — to be spiritually alert and to stand firm under pressure. The second two commands are offensive. To be courageous (in Greek, "to play the man"; "Quit ye like men" in the AV), suggests that the Christian life is a struggle. When Paul exhorts his readers to be strong, he is doing more than giving them a pep talk, for the strength of the believer does not rest in self-confidence but in the power of God, which is often displayed in great weakness.

Above all, as chapter 13 so beautifully proclaimed, they are to be guided by love. Even in the warfare for the truth and the right, love must be the governing principle.

### IV. Recognition of Leaders (16:15-18)

One of the problems in the Corinthian church was the failure to give due recognition to their leaders. Instead of accepting leadership, they rallied behind their favorite personalities. A half century later, Clement of Rome wrote a letter to the Corinthians, exhorting them again to respect their leaders.

Among their leaders was Stephanas and his household (v. 15). These were Paul's first converts in Achaia (that is the meaning of "firstfruits" here) and he had baptized them (1:16). Since Athens lay in the province of Achaia they may have moved to Corinth, for it was here that they had devoted themselves to the service of the saints.

It is sometimes argued that the New Testament teaches the baptism of children, since we have several household conversions. But our text militates against that view; baptized babes don't give themselves to Christian service.

One should point out that they did not wait until they were elected into a church committee before they began to serve, but they found occasions to minister without being asked or told. We need not blame the church when we feel our gifts are being neglected; if we have gifts, surely there is a place in our community where these can be put to good use.

To "know" the household of Stephanas does not mean simply to get to know members of this family (which may have included slaves), but to respect them. Even more, the Corinthians are "to be subject to such men and to every fellow worker and laborer" (v. 16). Not their status or their position demanded respect, but their function. Elsewhere Paul exhorts churches to esteem their leaders "for the sake of their work" (I Thess. 5:12ff.). Those who devoted themselves to the work of the Lord deserve the love, the care and the respect of the church.

It is easy to overlook this aspect of the life of the church. When "brotherhood" is understood to mean that we are all so equal that we submit to no one and fail to acknowledge the fact that God does give the church leaders, we do not model the teachings of Jesus or the apostles.

Perhaps the reference to the household of Stephanas reminded Paul to say a word of appreciation about Stephanas and his two companions, Achaicus and Fortunatus (v. 17). This Corinthian delegation may have brought the letter from Corinth, as well as some oral information. Paul had rejoiced at their coming, for they made up for the absence of the Corinthians — a tender touch indicating how dear these "problem children" were to his heart.

This breath of Corinth had refreshed his spirit. No doubt these men had often refreshed the Corinthians, also. Perhaps just to see such men of the faith, to have them around for a while, was a pleasure. (Some Christians, even leaders, can be difficult to have around.) In any case, people like this Corinthian delegation must be esteemed (v. 18).

## V. Final Salutations (16:19-24)

(a) *Greetings from Others* (vv. 19,20). Ephesus, where Paul served at the moment, was in the Roman province of Asia (modern
Turkey). During his ministry in this metropolis the gospel
penetrated this province (cf. Acts 19:10). These young churches
wanted Paul to convey their greetings to the Corinthians. Where
the relationship of believers is warm, such greetings are very
meaningful.

Aquila and Priscilla (usually mentioned in reverse order) had
left for Corinth when Claudius expelled the Jews from Rome.
There a working partnership with Paul developed and when Paul
left Corinth they settled in Ephesus (Acts 18:18ff.). Their house
served as a meeting place for at least part of the Ephesian church.
Later they were hosts to a Roman congregation (Rom. 16:3-5). This
dedicated couple, who had become the mentors of Apollos and had
risked their lives for Paul (Rom. 16:4), also send greetings with
their congregation as do Paul's missionary associates in Ephesus
("all the brethren with me," v. 20).

Paul exhorts the Corinthians to greet one another with a holy
kiss — the customary greeting of Paul's day. Whether the kiss had
already entered the church's liturgy, as it eventually did, is not certain. The form of the greeting is determined largely by cultural
practice but a "holy" kiss suggests there is an added dimension
when Christians shake hands, embrace, rub noses or kiss.

(b) *Greetings from Paul* (vv. 21-24). Evidently Paul had dictated
this letter, as was his practice, but he now takes the pen from the
hand of his secretary and writes a few closing lines in his own hand
writing (v. 21). Those who have no affection for Christ, he warns,
are accursed (v. 22).

Only here in the New Testament has the Aramaic *maranatha*
been retained and Paul doesn't bother to translate it into Greek.
Evidently it was a well-known invocation which the Greek-
speaking churches took over, as they did some other Semitic words
(e.g. Amen, Hallelujah, etc.). It means, "Our Lord, come"! In the
*Didache* (x. 6), a second century Christian document, *maranatha* appears as a eucharistic prayer, asking the Lord to be present at the
Lord's Table. However, as Revelation 22:20 clearly indicates, it is

also a plea for Christ to return and take his church home with him.

Paul began his letter by wishing his readers the fullness of God's grace, and he ends it on the same note (v. 23). This is more than a mere convention; Paul knows that the church lives, labors and survives only by God's grace. He closes his epistle on a very tender note: "My love be with you all in Christ Jesus" (v. 24).

### Personal Response

1. Paul encouraged the Christians at Corinth to give financial assistance to their fellow believers (vv. 1-4). In spite of some economic difficulties, North American Christians live affluent lives. How should this impact our financial stewardship? How can we help those facing economic difficulties among us?

2. Many readers have conditioned themselves to live on tight schedules. How can we be good stewards of our time and yet allow for the spontaneous leading of God?

3. Paul urged the Corinthians to recognize and respect the leaders among them (v. 16). How well do we do this in the church today? What are some areas in which we do not follow this command? How can we show respect and recognition for leaders?

4. In several of Paul's writings, he closes with greetings to individuals and churches. What does this say about relationships with others in the Christian family?

## Commentaries on I Corinthians
(Selected Bibliography)

Barclay, W. *The Letters to the Corinthians*. Philadelphia: Westminster Press, 1956.

Barrett, C.K. *The First Epistle to the Corinthians*. *London:* Adam and Charles Black, 1968.

Bruce, F.F. *I and II Corinthians*. London: Oliphants, 1971.

Conzelmann, H. *A Commentary on the First Epistle to the Corinthians*. Trans. by J.W. Leitch, et al. Philadelphia: Fortress Press.

deBoor, W. *Der erste Brief an die Korinther*. Wuppertal: R. Brockhaus Verlag, 1974.

Grosheide, F.W. *Commentary on the First Epistle to the Corinthians*. Grand Rapids: Eerdmans, 1953.

Hering, Jean. *The First Epistle of Saint Paul to the Corinthians*. Trans. by A.W. Heathcote and P.J. Allcock. London: Epworth, 1962.

Morris, L. *The First Epistle of Paul to the Corinthians*. Grand Rapids: Eerdmans, 1958.

Orr, W.F. and Walther, J.A. *I Corinthians*. The Anchor Bible. Garden City, N.Y.: Doubleday and Co., 1976.

Robertson, A. and Plummer, *A. A Critical and Exegetical Commentary on the First Epistle of St. Paul to the Corinthians*.ICC. Edinburgh: T. and T. Clark, 1914.

Wendland, H.D. *Die Briefe an die Korinther*. NT Deutsch. Goettingen: Vandenhoeck und Ruprecht, 1968 (12. Aufl.).